101

WAYS TO REDUCE PLASTIC

You can too

By
Kim Grove

I Found 101 Ways to Reduce Plastic You can too

First print edition

ISBN-13

You should direct requests to publish work from this book
to Kim Grove via:
http://www.kimgrove.co.uk/contact/

Cover designed by Briony Cousins

Printed by Amazon KDP Print

For David, with love
xxxx

Table of Contents

Introduction

I first became aware of the problem with plastic whilst watching David Attenborough in *Blue Planet II*. Soon afterwards, I went to a viewing of *A Plastic Ocean* at our local cinema. How was it possible to have all that plastic in the ocean? It showed plastic bags at the bottom of the deepest trenches, seabirds with endless amounts of plastic in their stomachs and ocean-going craft dropping all manner of debris into the sea. This wasn't right and I felt partly responsible. According to a report by Eunomia[1] *Plastics in the Marine Environment (2016),* 80% of the plastic in the sea comes from the land. There are estimates saying that there will be more plastic in the sea than fish by 2050!

I decided I had to do something, but this was minimal at first. Then came the TV programme *War on Plastic with Hugh and Anita*. This gave me lots of ideas of how I could reduce my own plastic use, and being a writer already, it gave me the enthusiasm to write about my progress.

This book explains what I did and offers suggestions of what you can try too.

---

[1] Eunomia is an independent consultancy dedicated to helping our clients to achieve better environmental and commercial outcomes.

Of course, plastic has its place. If it is reusable and can last a long time, I think it's acceptable, but I also think we should now stop manufacturing so much of it. There seems to be plenty already in circulation that can be recycled, surely we don't need any more.

In the three R's mantra of Reduce, Reuse, Recycle, there is a need to **reduce** the amount of plastic we use as the first step. If we do need to buy plastic, we need to reuse this as much as possible and phase out single-use plastic. Finally, when we've exhausted the other two, then we should recycle it and that means recycling **ALL** of it. That's the only way can we stop so much plastic reaching the ocean.

The current production of biodegradable plastic is rather low. Why is this? Shouldn't this be overtaking non-biodegradable plastic? I think though, that we have to be careful with the term 'biodegradable' as this can be misleading. Plastic is biodegradable, it's just that it takes hundreds of years to degrade. I think what we want to see here is a product that breaks down quickly (within months, if possible), and leaves no lasting particles to endanger the wildlife or our health.

Until this happens, and as far as possible, I wanted to use products that either didn't contain any (or very little) plastic, or change single-use into multi-use. I didn't succeed with everything, and in the future, I will be guided by your successes too. So, if you've found a plastic-free alternative, please let me know.

Unfortunately, supermarkets are not helping. They have taken to making their loose produce more expensive than plastic wrapped fruit and veg. This is ludicrous and I cannot understand their argument for this.

It forces us to buy the amount they want us to buy and not what we actually need (which is probably less). It doesn't help in our quest to buy just the right amount of food we need each week and could be one of the reasons for the vast quantities of food going to waste each year. According to WRAP (Waste and Resources Action Programme), we throw away 7 billion tonnes of food annually! And they say we can't feed the population of the world without genetically modified food. Really? Are the supermarkets' actions helping to increase waste?

In response, we've seen anarchy in the aisles. People have been ripping plastic packaging off food items, and leaving this for the supermarket to clear up (although I wouldn't be confident that they'd dispose of it correctly)!

A little more action wouldn't go amiss though.

One of the cheapest things we can do is to lobby. Consumers are powerful people! We can all make our voices heard by telling retailers what we want them to do. If you're fed up with your supermarket not having loose fruit and vegetables at a reasonable price, tell them so. It only takes an email, and a threat that you'll shop with their rivals until they've sorted this problem out.

Imagine if everyone in a small town got together and boycotted their supermarket until they sold the items in the way everyone wanted. What do you think would happen? The supermarket would have to change or they'd be out of business. That's how powerful we can be!

Reducing plastic is not cheap, mind! I would say that some of the products I've bought to are quite expensive and I think this needs to change to make the items more competitive, so that everyone can help to make a difference. For this reason, wherever I can I have offered a cheaper alternative that people could use instead.

During my drive to reduce plastic, I contacted many companies about their products, and asked what they were doing to lower the plastic their goods contained. Some of them gave me a load of old bunkum in response. So I either:

- Stopped using their products – firing back a quick email to say, "Thanks for the information. I'll shop with you again when you've stopped using plastic in your product!"
- Ignored them and changed the product.
- Or if I was particularly irked with the way they had responded to my first email, I contacted them again, calling them to account for their response.

I doubt that these companies would be happy for me to quote them word for word, so I've précised their responses instead. If these companies don't think I've been fair, I'm happy for them to get back to me and update me on where they are with their plastic reduction and to give me a quote to upload.

I am based in the UK and many of the stockists are from the UK too (a few are international); however the principles within the book will apply to other countries. You will have local supermarkets, farmers markets and stockists selling similar products. If you know of a product in your country similar to those mentioned within this book, let me know and I can feature them in any updates.

A note here about aluminium.
Within this book, there will be some mentions of aluminium or aluminium foil, and whilst this is an alternative to plastic, it is not a good environmental alternative. It takes huge amounts of energy to produce aluminium, adding unwanted carbon into the atmosphere.

I rarely use this, but if I buy aluminium foil, I use If You Care foil, a recycled brand that takes a lot less energy to produce. None of the local supermarkets sell this. Luckily, my local refill shop does, so I either buy it from there or purchase it from Amazon.

Chapter 1
Reducing Plastic in the Kitchen

There's an awful lot of plastic in the kitchen. Almost half of all the plastic produced is used for packaging and most of that is to wrap supermarket food. For some strange reason, we have allowed these stores to get away with this. Why? We're the customers, and we are incredibly powerful people. Without our business, the supermarkets won't survive, so we need to tell them loudly and clearly, that the amount of plastic they use for packaging is not acceptable. The way we buy food is the key to solving this problem.

Buying Food

Before we get started on the reductions I've made, I wanted to share my food philosophy with you as this explains how I've manged to reduce so much food plastic. This doesn't mean that I expect you to follow me, or that I'm right, but I've tried to find ways to be more environmentally sustainable when it comes to food.

I buy organic food where possible. I feel that organic food is better for the environment. As there is very little (or no) use of chemicals either as fertiliser or as pesticide. This means that run-off from fields doesn't pollute the surrounding waterways and local wildlife thrives in the hedgerows surrounding the fields. The organic system doesn't allow general antibiotic use for meat-producing animals, and so this doesn't contribute to the global rise in antibiotic resistance. The way the farmer manages the fields and soil means that the produce has a higher amount of nutrients than conventional produce. According to NurtitionFacts.org (and backed up by the Soil Association), organic fruit and vegetables have between 19% and 65% more antioxidants than conventionally grown food, making the organic food 20% to 40% healthier.

I shop in my local Waitrose. I know some consider this shop expensive, but it sells a large range of organic produce thanks to its association with Prince Charles' Duchy range. It has also trialled and widened out a refill service, which is good news, as this should save people money as well as plastic. I don't think Waitrose goes far enough in terms of the organic produce on offer and I've had many an email conversation (and a verbal discussion) about this. However, it has certainly done a lot to reduce its plastic and even has a Plastic Plan – *Taking Action on Plastics* (2019) which it says it will update annually. This explains what it has done or is doing to reduce the plastic it uses. Moreover, I have noticed changes in-store. I'll tell you about these where relevant within the text of this book.

As for the 'expensiveness', I did a little experiment many years ago, shopping with a so-called 'cheaper' supermarket, only to find my shopping bill £20 higher each week. After a month, I returned to shop at Waitrose, and have never looked back.

Of course, you will use the supermarket you prefer. If it doesn't have what you want, or has what you don't want, i.e. plastic wrapped food, then tell the manager this. The more that people express their views, the more they will listen. Moreover, if they don't listen, you have the option of voting with your feet and taking your hard-earned cash to a supermarket that does listen to you. Don't forget to tell the supermarket that you have abandoned them and the reasons for this!

I also shop with Abel and Cole. This online organic supermarket offers meat, fish, fruit and vegetable boxes (and combinations of these) as well as a nice range of pantry items. I'm not keen on the Monday delivery but its minimum spend is only £12.00 (with a £1.50 delivery charge) so it's a good option. Although its range is limited, it was a godsend during the coronavirus pandemic as I was able to buy meat, fish and pantry items from them after Riverford stopped selling most items.

I buy my fruit, vegetables and eggs from Riverford. I used to buy meat and pantry items from them too. However, during the pandemic it decided to take many items off sale, which left me in difficulty. I'll be using Abel and Cole for these products in the future.

Riverford is also a company selling organic fruit and vegetable boxes, although you can usually buy individual items too as long as you have a minimum spend of £15. Delivery is free. It delivers fruit and vegetables (mainly) loose in a cardboard box, which I return each week, and the company reuses this up to 10 times. The delivery comes on a Thursday (which suits me better), although just like Abel and Cole, the delivery day depends on where you live.

I did a quick experiment to see how supermarket prices compared with Riverford. Taking a list of Riverford's box contents for the week (eight items), I took the price of 100 g for each individually priced item and compared each one to the 100 g equivalent organic price in Waitrose, Sainsbury's, Tesco, Asda and Abel and Cole. Where there was no equivalent, I used the Riverford price. You can see the results below:

Riverford	£19.30
Waitrose	£18.79 (two items missing)
Sainsbury's	£18.50 (same two items missing)
Asda	£16.67 (four items missing)
Abel and Cole	£19.47 (one item missing)

I didn't include Tesco as it only had three of the basket items in organic form in its online shop (and very little organic choice).

Although the two box-scheme organisations came in more expensive for individual items, the boxes were much cheaper. Able and Cole's medium box that week was £16.50 (so cheaper than the supermarkets) as opposed to Riverford's medium box at £14.95, which beat all the stores here.

At Christmas, Riverford also offers an entire Christmas

dinner box (including turkey, all the vegetables, pigs in blankets, stuffing, cranberry sauce, Christmas pudding, Mince pies, satsumas, etc.), which is cheaper than buying the individual items on offer.

I buy fish from the local farmers' market. Farmers' markets are much more popular than they used to be, although our local market seems to be dwindling off a bit lately. I'll talk more about fish later in the book.

Vegetables

Reduction No. 1
As all the supermarkets' organic produce comes wrapped in plastic, I use Riverford to keep me in vegetables with very little plastic. I can either buy one of their pre-determined boxes, which is what I've been doing lately. This contains whatever vegetables they have available, which forces me to cook and eat seasonally as well. Or I can choose individual vegetables to make up my own box, as long as I spend the minimum £15 each time I order (although the company removed this option during the coronavirus outbreak). Moreover, it is left in the place I want it if I'm out – usually by my back door.

Most of the vegetables come loose within the box, but for those that might be prone to damage, such as tomatoes and mushrooms, the company packs them in a paper tray, although loose items like salad leaves, still come in a plastic bag.

Riverford is looking reduce all plastic packaging by the end of 2020. Its website says, *"There are many different types [of biodegradable and compostable plastics] on the market, and some are worse for the environment than conventional plastic. As well as being non-recyclable, they require high temperatures to break down, meaning they don't biodegrade if they end up in landfill or in the ocean."* As an alternative, the company is aiming to introduce certified home compostable packaging instead for its punnets and bags.

A while back, I noticed that when I ordered large quantities of tomatoes and mushrooms, these came in plastic punnets rather than paper trays. I wondered why Riverford couldn't just put the larger quantities into bigger paper trays. So I emailed the company to find out the reason for this. I also pointed out that it was also cheaper to buy the products in these sizes.

Customer relations came back to me and said that paper trays were not available in larger sizes and because the sales of these were so small, a change in their packaging supplier wasn't viable. They apologised about the price difference between smaller and larger punnets, but reiterated that Riverford was switching all its punnets over to 100% home compostable packaging by the end of the year.

I'll have to wait for this instead. Until then, I've reduced the quantity I order so that I get compostable boxes!

These days, supermarkets sometimes offer vegetables in polystyrene trays, and whilst this isn't plastic, it's made from the same constituents as plastic so it might as well be, as this too is polluting the oceans, and takes just as long to break down.

Polystyrene manufacturers would have you believe you can recycle this product, particularly 'expanded' polystyrene, which you could if recycling collectors accepted it, which they don't, and if it was sent for recycling, which it isn't.

In the 'old' days, people used to take a bag into the greengrocer, and would receive their potatoes, carrots, onions, cabbage, etc., straight into the bag. As supermarkets now charge for their plastic bags (or do away with them altogether in some cases), we've become much better at taking our own recycled bags with us, and you can try this too. Keep one or two bags for loose, possibly muddy, fruit and vegetables.

There is another alternative. You can buy your produce from a market or greengrocer, where you can often buy as much or little loose fruit and veg as you want.

Reduction No. 2
If I have to go into a supermarket to buy vegetables, I now take the vegetables out of the plastic wrapping, and leave this on the shelf for the supermarket to clear up.

Why not take your produce out of the plastic packaging, put the loose vegetables into your own bag and leave the plastic waste with the supermarket. Maybe they'll get the message and provide a much larger range of (if not all) loose vegetables in the very near future!

Reduction No. 3

I grow some of my own vegetables, and amazingly, these don't grow covered in plastic! They are also organic, as I use my own compost and no chemicals. This means each year, I reduce my plastic even further as French beans, rocket and lettuce to name but a few things, still come in plastic from Riverford. I use organic seed wrapped in paper and foil, plastic seed trays (which I've had for many years), and my own compost (already mentioned) within the pots and on the beds.

This year I'm growing tomatoes, cucumber, courgettes, beans – runner, French and broad, carrots, parsnips (although these are not looking great) and many more.

Why not have a go at growing your own. If you don't have a garden, you can plant a few veg in containers and put them onto a balcony or outside your front or back door. You just need a bit of compost and a few seeds. It's a bit quicker if you can buy seedlings from your local garden centre. Sometimes you can even find these at garden gates or fetes.

Fruit

I've had the same problems with fruit as with vegetables.

As I wander down the fruit aisle of my local supermarket, fruit wrapped in plastic outweighs loose fruit by a considerable margin, and this is even worse with organic fruit, as none comes without plastic. I can also see lemons and limes in plastic nets.

Reduction No. 4
I buy my fruit from Riverford. I have a large fruit box delivered every week (except when there is an abundance of apples and pears in the garden, when I reduce my order to a few loose items). The fruit box contains five varieties (we like fruit in our house), usually apples and bananas, and three other seasonal fruits. The fruit is organic and there is quite a variety to choose from if I want to buy extra loose. Soft fruit comes in paper trays for protection, which are compostable – they go into my compost bin in the garden.

Reduction No. 5
Unlike the supermarkets, the lemons and limes from Riverford, come in a net which is made of compostable beech material, so no plastic nets at Riverford.

Of course, one way you can reduce plastic fruit packaging is to buy from a greengrocer, market, local farm shop or use a box scheme instead. There are lots of these springing up around the country now.

Also, and especially during the summer, you can still find fruit farms where you can pick your own fruit and I often see people selling seasonal fruit in lay-bys from the back of their car.

If you start to buy your 'plastic-free' fruit from elsewhere, don't forget to let your supermarket know that you have done this. Tell them why they have lost your custom and what they need to do to get this back. If everyone did this, supermarkets would have no option but to change their practice or risk going bust!

Fruit stickers

Reduction No. 6

I've been doing some research into those annoying little plastic stickers that infect supermarket fruit. The damn things are so fiddly to get off, especially if you forget to take them off before washing the fruit. Who wants to eat glue, edible or otherwise? These stickers are one of the reasons I stopped buying loose fruit and vegetables from the supermarket.

Do we need them? Well, no. The stickers contain three things:

1. A description of what the item is! Hmm, I think I know if it's a lemon, an apple, or a banana so I don't think I need them to tell me this on a tiny sticker.

2. Details about where it comes from, which is marginally more helpful, if I'm interested in why my apple comes from halfway around the world in September, when we grow perfectly good apples in the UK at that time of year. Anyway, the supermarket usually puts this onto the price label.

3. The registration number or PLU code (price look-up). This is supposed to tell you whether it was grown conventionally or organically or whether it has been

genetically modified.

I looked one of these codes up. A lemon, code 4033 from Chile. It told me this was indeed a lemon, that its botanical name was 'Citrus limon' (it should say Citrus x limon, if you want to be botanically correct, but hey it's close enough), and the size was small – less than 54mm – hmm – I think I can see how big or small it is!

You and I don't need this information. So it's about time supermarkets removed these, not us. I remove these from fruit and leave them in the supermarket. If we all did this, maybe they'd get fed up with cleaning them up and lobby for their removal!

Herbs and spices

Herbs
I love herbs and spices and use them a lot. They finish a dish off, making it warming and comforting in winter, fresh, and vibrant in the summer.

Reduction No. 7
I grow organic herbs in the garden. This means I've stopped buying herbs in little plastic bags from the supermarket.

Most of the herbs in my garden are evergreen, like bay, thyme, rosemary and sage (good for soups and stews in the winter) or are perennial, coming back year after year, like mint. The perennial herbs are seasonal, but it doesn't seem right using mint in the winter anyway.

If the herb plants don't look great after the ravages of winter, I'll compost the old ones and buy a new herb plant, either from the Organic Garden Catalogue (if I'm ordering something else at the time) or from the local nursery. Some of them I'll grow from seed, which I do anyway each year for basil and coriander as these are the herbs I use most in summer. It's good to have a ready supply.

You could do the same. Herbs are lovely grown in places where you can brush past them and release their scent as you walk along a pathway or the edge of the patio (lavender, rosemary and thyme are good for this). Alternatively, pop them into your borders amongst your usual flowers or plants, especially in a place close to where you sit so you can enjoy their scent.

If you don't have a garden, why not keep a few pots of herbs on your windowsill or balcony. Easy to grow herbs include basil, chives, coriander (although this also goes to seed quickly) and parsley. Don't buy herb plants in black pots though as these are difficult to recycle (more about this in the meat section).

Reduction No. 8
I have very few dried organic herbs in my kitchen cupboard. Thyme, oregano and rosemary are the only ones I use, and this mostly in winter. However, when these run out, I need to replace them. I could buy herbs from the supermarket. These come in a box, which is great, but inside the box, the company has put the herbs into a plastic packet – not so

great.

Because of this, I buy my herbs either directly from Steenbergs, which sells organic herbs and spices in glass jars with stainless steel tops or I order them from Abel and Cole if I have a delivery coming from them.

My local refill shop, Refill Revolution, also sells loose herbs and spices, which could be an alternative, but as these are not organic, I don't buy them. If they stock organic herbs in the future, I will definitely buy from them.

Spices
Reduction No. 9
Where possible, I buy fresh spices, which is easy for items such as garlic, chillies, ginger, turmeric and lemon grass. I used to buy these from the supermarket but as Riverford sell these, I buy from them. The company delivers these in a compostable beech net or brown paper bag.

I have also grown my own varieties of these (except for turmeric), which of course, you can try yourself. It's very satisfying to have a string of chillies hanging in the kitchen over the winter period that you have grown and threaded yourself. It also makes a nice gift for a chilli fan!

However, for other, more exotic spices, such as cinnamon, star anise or pepper, growing them is not so easy, which is why I have a cupboard full of dried spices. As with herbs, most of these come from Steenbergs, not only because they are organic, but also because they come in glass containers with stainless steel lids.

Meat

I generally buy my meat from three sources:

1. Abel and Cole
2. Riverford
3. Waitrose – as a last resort – and if I can find any organic meat (which often I can't).

There is a major problem with these companies' meat supplies, and that is that they still use plastic trays, with plastic film coverings for their meat packaging.

Abel and Cole say that I can wash and recycle its plastic trays for meat (and fish). However, the film lid is not widely recycled. It suggests that if we have a local TerraCycle® collection point we should take the lid there. I'll look into this.

Riverford uses clear trays into which it packs its meat, or alternatively, it uses a vacuumed plastic wrap. It seems to have done something recently so that the film covering comes off the top of the chicken trays cleanly, making it easier to recycle the tray.

I emailed Riverford to ask what they were doing about its plastic meat trays and it old me that there were no plans to change the way they packed meat as it is subject to food safety regulations. Although they conceded that they may look into meat packaging in the future.

Waitrose has a lot of information about how it intends to reduce plastic in its Plastic Plan. The plan said it was going to remove the black plastic it packaged meat into, as a priority. This is because there is a problem with the sensors at recycling plants as these can't detect the dark pigment in the plastic. This means that although the black plastic trays were recyclable, they weren't being recycled and were ending up in landfill instead causing more pollution. This is a promise that Waitrose has fulfilled, as it no longer seems to use black plastic for its meat and poultry (fish too).

Of course, there is the supermarket meat counter or a butcher that can provide plastic-free packaging. Waitrose is happy to put meat, fish and deli items into the customer's own containers. Unfortunately, neither of my local shops offer organic meat at the moment.

Reduction No. 10
My solution to reducing plastic wrapped meat is that I hardly ever buy meat now and so my consumption of plastic meat wrapping has decreased considerably.

Why not pay your local butcher or the meat counter at your local supermarket a visit and take your own multi-use boxes to these shops to put the meat into directly.

Alternatively, if you haven't already done so, you could change your diet to a meat free (or reduced meat) one.

Fish

I buy my fish from the fishmonger at the local farmers'

market. I've been shopping from the 'fish-man' for six or seven years now. He actually catches the fish in the week, and then sells this at our local market. He gives lots of information about the state of fish stocks and any fish stock closures. He prepares the fish any way you want it. For example, he'll take the head off, gut it or fillet it and he's even shown me how to 'prepare' a squid, cutting the beak out and removing the entrails and quill.

His wife, who accompanies him to the market, makes all the fish pies (which come in a foil tray), fish-cakes (which he places in a papier mâché box and fish chowders (contained in a recyclable plastic tub) and which are a delight.

Reduction No. 11

I buy enough fish for the month and freeze this. The fishmonger usually wraps the fish in paper, which is compostable, and I used to place the paper-wrapped fish inside a plastic bag to stop this leaking or smelling whilst in the freezer, but I've stopped doing that now. Instead, I have a large plastic click and lock container that I put the fish into and then put the whole lot into the freezer. This, therefore, replaces the single-use plastic I've used in the past. I'm in the process of sorting out my plastic containers to see whether there are any suitable that he can put the fish into directly.

Why not take your own containers to your local fishmonger or supermarket wet-fish counter, and ask them to put your purchases straight into these.

Dairy

Milk

We used to drink organic UHT skimmed milk in our house. Unfortunately, this milk only comes in cartons and these contain plastic, so is not preferable.

My husband likes to drink milk, and so we would buy semi-skimmed milk in plastic containers from the supermarket. Again, not an environmentally friendly option.

Reduction No. 12

To counter this, we have signed up to a regular milk home delivery service. The company delivers organic milk twice a week and of course, this comes in recyclable glass bottles with a recyclable aluminium lid. We have just changed the company, so I don't know what they will be like just yet, so haven't included them in the list of stockists.

You could find out whether there is a local home milk delivery service or farm shop that will supply your milk. They often sell other items too, which could save you a trip to the supermarket.

Yogurt
Reduction No. 13

I used to buy packs of four individual plain yogurts and eat one with my lunch. I read somewhere that if you buy individual cartons, there is more plastic in these than if you buy the equivalent amount of yogurt in a larger carton. So I started buying the larger container of yogurt and decanting this into reusable plastic tubs to take to work, reducing my single-use plastic consumption.

Reduction No. 14
However, this got me thinking, why don't I make my own yogurt. I used to do this when we had a smallholding. I don't know what happened to the old yogurt maker, so I've invested in a new one that comes with individual glass jars in which I make the yogurt. This is cheaper, as I only pay for the milk (okay and the electricity), but this way, I get to control how much sugar or fruit goes into each jar – if any! I can then just take a small jar with me to work, instead of decanting the yogurt into a smaller pot, and bring this home to put it into the dishwasher ready for the next time. I can even make the next round of yogurt from the previous batch.

If you buy yogurt in larger containers you'll also find this cheaper than smaller ones, so this is a good option if you don't want to make your own. But making your own without a machine is also easy and cheaper than buying it.

If you want to have a go at making your own, here is a quick and easy method for you to try. Heat a thermos flask with hot water (leave the water inside until you are ready to pour in the mixture, then throw the water away or use it for something else). Heat 2 pints (1 litre) of milk (whole milk is best but any will work) into a pan and heat until it is just about to boil. Leave this to cool until you can put your finger in without burning it, but is still hot. Whilst the milk is cooling, put 2 tablespoons of live yogurt into a jug. When the milk is ready, add a little to the yogurt and stir together gently until mixed. Add the rest of the milk and mix together. Pour into the flask and leave for 8 hours after which time this should have turned into yogurt.

You can experiment with different types and quantities of milk. You can put any fruit you like in when it's ready. You can also make the next batch of yogurt from this one.

Butter
Reduction No. 15
I usually buy Yeo Valley butter from Waitrose. We use two sorts of butter in our house. Block butter, for making bread (and cakes if the fancy takes me) and spreadable butter for putting on toast or making sandwiches. The tubs that the spreadable butter comes in are recyclable, so I put these into the kerbside recycling bin to be re-fashioned into fleeces, pillows, new plastic bottles, etc.

I was unsure whether the wrappings were actually recyclable, so I wrote to the company to find out. It confirmed that the spreadable butter packaging is recyclable, but not the block butter wrap. This contains layers of greaseproof paper with an outer layer of aluminium foil and a layer of LDPE (plastic) between the two. These are not recyclable, as the fat from the butter has contaminated the greaseproof paper, so it's unable to make it through the recycling process. The company did suggest I compost the greaseproof paper layer, so I will give this a go.
I have since found an alternative to the block butter. Both Riverford and Abel and Cole sell unsalted butter blocks,

which are organic and wrapped in compostable paper. I now buy this from whoever delivers the next order.

Custard
Reduction No. 16
I used to buy tubs of custard (wrapped in plastic), mainly because it's fiddly to make 'real' custard (or crème anglaise to give it its proper name), without it splitting. I've now come to a compromise; I use custard powder and make my own version of custard.

There is a person at our local farmers' market that makes crème anglaise and puts it into a jar, but you have to use it quickly as it contains eggs and it doesn't freeze, so I have to time it just right!

Cakes and biscuits

I don't eat sweets, and only eat the occasional cake or biscuit. If I buy these, which I have done in the past, they usually come in plastic packaging and if they come in a box, there is usually an internal plastic window.

Reduction No. 17
I therefore don't buy these anymore, and will make my own from time to time, particularly if we are having people to stay over the weekend. Using my food processor, they don't take long to make, and they cook in next to no time. You can also control or reduce the amount of sugar that goes into these (most recipes – even jam – can cope with less sugar), or I'll replace it altogether with fruit that is naturally sweet.

Why not make your own biscuits. I have a recipe that I adapt for all my biscuits then I add dried fruit and layer it (like Garibaldi biscuits), add peanuts (or other nuts) for nutty cookies, or layer two biscuits together with buttercream or jam.

Beat together 200 g (7 oz) soft butter and 120 g (4 oz) sugar (caster is better but not essential) in a mixing bowl. Add 1 egg yolk and beat into the mixture. If you want to add flavourings such as vanilla, lemon juice or orange juice, add 2 teaspoons of it at this point. This is a good time to add in nuts, fruit, oats etc. too. Sift 400 g (14 oz) plain flour into the mixing bowl and fold into the mixture until combined. It needs to be quite a firm paste. You could bring the dough together with your hands. That's it. Shape in whatever way you want. Cook these in the oven at 200C / 180C fan / gas 6 for 10-15 minutes.

Plastic wrapped convenience foods

This depends on what you call a convenience food, whether you eat any of these and of course, if they are wrapped in plastic, which many are.

Pasta
I'd call this a convenience food, as you can make your own pasta – if you have the inclination – and a pasta machine – I've had three of these now, and each of them have ended up at the charity shop. I now buy dried pasta!
Reduction No. 18
Unfortunately, dried pasta usually comes wrapped in plastic. The good thing is that Refill Revolution now sells

loose organic pasta in penne, spiral and spaghetti versions, so I buy dried pasta from there now. I take a reusable plastic click and lock container to the shop for them to fill up.

Rice
Reduction No. 19
Is rice a convenience food? I'm not sure where else to put this otherwise. Anyway, it usually comes wrapped in plastic. Apparently, rice production is bad for the environment. The water that the rice grows in produces large quantities of bacteria, which releases methane into the atmosphere, and this is 80 times greater than carbon dioxide as a greenhouse gas. Wow!

However, I do buy rice every one to two months. Until recently, my local refill shop did not stock organic basmati rice, but it does now, so I buy this from them instead of the supermarket. Again, I take in a click and lock container for them to fill up for me.

Tomato ketchup
Reduction No. 20
I used to buy the squeezy bottles of Heinz organic tomato ketchup (although I didn't like having to wipe around nozzle). I've now replaced this with Mr Organic ketchup, which comes in a glass bottle with a recyclable cap. It tastes much more tomatoey as well, which is a bonus.

Drinks

Water
Reduction No. 21
This is a weird story that I can't get my head around!

For some reason, millions of people happily pay over the odds for water that comes out of the tap at a fraction of the price. More importantly, most of this comes in a plastic bottle, although I did go somewhere recently where all the water for sale was in aluminium cans – but as we now know, manufacturers' line these cans with plastic too.

I stopped buying water in bottles when I heard a chap on the TV saying it was the equivalent of going into a pub and paying £2,000 for a pint of beer. Who would do such a thing? Not that I drink beer, but even I can appreciate the economics of this.

I don't buy water, except for that which comes out of my tap. If I want to take water out with me, I used to fill up a multi-use plastic bottle with its own built-in straw (I'm not sure how hygienic these stay over time, and they seem to degrade quite quickly too). More latterly, I use a beautiful Chilly as a water carrier that my lovely niece gave to me for my birthday.

This is an easy one to try. There are lots of water carriers on the market at all different prices, and you only need to buy this once. Alternatively, if you have an old pop bottle or thermos flask, just wash it out and use that instead.

Reduction No. 22

Just about the only 'fizzy' drink (or mixer) I buy is tonic water, which I used to drink as an alternative to tea. Occasionally (Christmas), I buy lemonade or coke for visitors. However, I was ill last Christmas for a couple of weeks, and I just wanted to drink water. When I went to drink tonic again, I found it far too sweet, so I've now stopped drinking it preferring water instead.

I now only add tonic to the odd shot of gin – I do like a gin and tonic every so often and I've started to buy small glass bottles of tonic instead of the usual plastic ones. This again reduces the amount of single-use plastic I buy.

Reduction No. 23

My husband drinks beer, and used to buy the multi-packs. You know the ones that come with the rings that keep the cans together in 4's or 6's. However, after seeing some of the sea life with these rings around their necks, I've banned them from the house.

Luckily, his new favourite beer comes in bottles, which you buy individually.

My husband's second favourite beer comes from a local brewer and these are also bottled and wrapped in a card holder, although you can also buy single bottles directly from them. They also offer small barrels that they will refill and although these are plastic, they are not single use as my husband has these refilled every now and again.

Beverages

Tea

I drink a lot of tea! It was Twinings originally, and this came in a cardboard box (which, for a change, didn't have a plastic covering). The teabags inside were packed in a foil bag, although I wasn't convinced that this didn't contain plastic.

According to the Tea Council in the UK, we make 96% of all tea with a teabag, so I wanted to know what teabags were made from. I did some research and what a minefield it was. There is a lot of conflicting information about tea on the internet, so I emailed Twinings to ask them about their tea and their packaging.

The upshot is that their teabags contain a plastic based material (acrylic polymer binder), which is used to bind the paper together. In addition, the teabags contain polypropylene fibres, which enable the producer to seal them together so they don't fall apart when we swish them around in the cup.

Twinings also told me that the foil wrapper that keeps the teabags fresh inside the box is not recyclable either, although it is looking into alternative materials for this. However, the company does say that it is trialling fully biodegradable teabags across all its ranges, as a means of being kinder to the planet.

So, Twinings teabags are currently made of plastic but are

hoping to change sometime in the future.

Reduction No. 24

So what did I do? I switched brands to a one that doesn't contain plastic. I now buy Clipper teabags instead. According to its website, it makes its teabags from:

"A blend of abaca (a species of banana), plant cellulose fibres and PLA – a bio-polymer derived from non-GM plant material."

The English Breakfast and Earl Grey versions are rather nice. The only problem is that there is no Lady Grey (as that is a Twinings blend). However, Clipper does do a white tea with orange that is similar, and it's lovely, although it's not Lady Grey!

The main problem I have is that local supermarkets don't stock Clipper tea, so I have to buy these directly from the company, which means I have to pay a delivery charge on top of the price of the tea. I can get it from Amazon, but it's about the same price. I've therefore started buying this in bulk.

Why not check out your tea brand to see whether it contains plastic and if it does switch it. In the UK, the following teabags in addition to Clipper are plastic-free: those from Abel & Cole, the Co-op own brand 99, Pukka tea, Teapigs, Twinings pyramid range and Waitrose Duchy range.

Coffee
Reduction No. 25
I don't drink coffee, but my husband does and so do many of the people who come and visit. We used to buy jars of coffee, but unfortunately, if you look at the coffee selection on the supermarket shelves, although there are plenty of glass jars, these all seem to have plastic lids.

This was until my husband found Nespresso. He's now the proud owner of a Nespresso coffee machine and so uses Nespresso capsules, which are made of aluminium (we've covered aluminium before), but luckily no plastic. He also collects the pods and returns them to the company for recycling, which, according to their website, they recycle to make new capsules. Although it does say '*where feasible*', so I'm not sure to what extent this actually happens. My husband now offers everyone a coffee or cappuccino from 'his' machine.

Does your coffee product contain plastic packaging? If it does, you could always write to the company and ask them to switch to non-plastic.

Hot chocolate
I buy and drink hot chocolate, which is a bit weird, as I don't like chocolate – I don't mind the taste but not the texture. I think I like hot chocolate as this is usually quite sweet and comforting, but I don't like it when it's made from chocolate!

I buy hot chocolate powder that you just add water to

rather than milk, mainly because its quick and I don't have to get a pan out to heat the milk (I don't have a microwave).

I use Clipper instant hot chocolate, sadly not organic, because the organic version requires milk rather than water.

However, like all other hot chocolate drinks, this comes in a card container, with what looks like an aluminium base, but a plastic lid. It has no information on the side about how to recycle this, so I contacted the company who told me that the metal base and plastic lid can be recycled, but that the paper tub and metal seal can't be recycled as it contains a mixture of materials.

I feel I've failed in my plastic reduction here! Does anyone out there know of a plastic-free hot chocolate that I can make with water?

Preparing food

When I prepare food, I use plastic equipment and utensils, but I've had these items for many years (which shows how useful plastic can be at times).

I have plastic colour-coded chopping boards for hygiene purposes. I also use a plastic mixing bowl from time to time, although I tend to favour my metal and glass mixing bowls. I have plastic serving utensils (potato masher, ladle etc.) and spatulas for stirring food so these don't scratch my saucepans (although I also use wooden spoons and spatulas for this too) but these are all reusable.

Taking packed lunches to work

My husband and I both take packed lunches to work, which usually consists of:

- A sandwich or salad of some description
- A piece of fruit
- Some yogurt

Sandwiches and salads
Reduction No. 26
My husband very kindly makes my sandwiches for work each morning. He used to wrap these in clingfilm (see covering food in the fridge for more information on clingfilm). This was until I discovered If You Care Paper Snack and Sandwich Bags. The company makes the sandwich bags using pulp from FSC (Forest Stewardship Council) approved forests. They contain no petroleum, chemicals or plastics and are compostable and recyclable.

My hubby now puts our sandwiches into these instead. I bring the bags home and put the finished bag into the kitchen food waste bucket, which goes for municipal composting.

If I take a salad to work, I'll use a reusable plastic clip and lock container for this. I take dressings or mayonnaise separately in small screw-top plastic pots. These items are both reusable. I take a stainless steel knife and fork out of the drawer, so I don't use disposable plastic cutlery, then bring everything home to wash in the dishwasher when I do the evening wash.

Fruit

Fruit such as apples, pears and bananas don't need extra wrapping as the rind (or peel) provides its own protection. The only time I use a container is if I take some soft fruit like strawberries, raspberries or blueberries to work. I use a small reusable screw-top plastic container for these.

Storing food

To keep food fresh for as long as possible (and stop it going into the food waste bin), we need to store it properly. Bacteria multiply at a rapid rate. Each one divides into two every 15-20 minutes given the right growing conditions of food, warmth, moisture and time. The temperature at which bacteria multiply at is between 5°C and 63°C, although they will grow more quickly at body temperature of 37°C.

Therefore, your fridge needs to be at a temperature lower than this to make sure the bacteria can't multiply. So your fridge should be somewhere between 1°C and 4°C. Your freezer obviously needs to be cold enough to freeze the food and keep it frozen. So the temperature should be somewhere between -18°C and -25°C. If you are unsure about the temperatures of your fridge and freezer, you can buy a cheap thermometer and keep one in each appliance. They only cost about £1 each.

It's also important to put the food in the fridge in the right place. A useful guide is:

Top Shelf
- Eggs – keep these in their original boxes as they will keep for longer.
- Cheese, butter, yogurt and cream.
- Ready to eat food.

Middle Shelf
- Cooked meat.
- Leftover dishes.

Bottom Shelf
- Raw meat and poultry, fish and seafood. This is so that any juices that might drip from these products do not run onto cooked food (which should be above these items in the fridge). Keep the products in their original wrappings. I also put these onto a plate or bowl when defrosting for added protection.

Fridge Drawers
- Vegetables and salads items (wash before use).

Fridge Door
- Drinks, sauces, mustards, jams, pickles.

If you store food in the freezer, you should follow the manufacturer's instructions and star rating. This will tell you how long you can store each type of food (unfortunately, these are all different). As a general rule of thumb, only keep each food item in the freezer for about three months. You should also store tinned and dried food in a way that prevents contamination. For example, opened packets of cereal, can attract bugs and beasties, so seal these tightly with a clip or you could put the contents into a container with a secure lid.

Try not to buy damaged tins. If you are only using a small amount of food from the tin, tip the rest into a plastic or glass bowl, then cover and store in the fridge.

Covering food in the fridge

It's so easy to reach for clingfilm, to cover leftover food destined for the fridge. It's handy, cheap and quick to use (as long as you have one of these products with a blade that actually cuts the film)!

Apparently, in the UK we get through miles and miles of the stuff. According to the *Daily Mail*, UK households use more than 1.2 billion metres or 746 miles of it each year. That's enough to go round the world 30 times! Imagine how much we must use globally.

They make clingfilm mainly from polyvinyl chloride (PVC), which is not recyclable or biodegradable, so it usually ends up in landfill, where it accumulates polluting groundwater as the chemicals seep out. The broken down plastic can also float about in the air like smoke from a fire, polluting the surrounding environment too.

Because of this, I wanted to stop using clingfilm, but I had to find some alternatives first, and I found a few.

Bees wax wrap
Reduction No. 27
This is a sheet of cloth that has been soaked in beeswax, which enables you to mould it over bowls or food packets. I use this to cover cheese (it actually seems to make the cheese last a bit longer), and for covering bowls of food in the fridge.

It is becoming very popular, and I've managed to get a few people at work using this too. Several companies now produce this (Beeswax Wraps, Bee Green Wraps, and BeeBee Wraps). You can find this in a variety of shapes, sizes and colours. I use Bees Wrap®, which I first bought from Lakeland, but I see you can now buy this from Waitrose and Morrisons. Other supermarkets seem to be struggling to stock this clingfilm replacement! Of course, you could lobby them about this.

The downside is that they are not cheap, but they do last for up to a year. The cheapest I've found is £7.95 from Amazon, but these are coming down in price quite quickly. I've had mine for about a year now and the sheets are still going strong. They just need a wash in warm (not hot) soapy water, and left to dry naturally, and then you can fold them up and use them again. I keep the original card packet to store them in.

Beeswax is much cheaper to buy than the wraps. So if you purchase some of this or if you keep bees, you could make your own. You just need piece of material such as an old tea towel, then just melt the wax, dip the material in and leave this to dry.

Note: Use an old saucepan for melting the wax as it can be difficult to wash off afterwards.

Two plates or a plate over a bowl
Reduction No. 28
This is another way to reduce plastic when storing food in the fridge. Just recently, I've been using a plate top and bottom to cover food such as ham slices that I intend to use the next day, or I'll cover a bowl containing something like left over baked beans, with a small plate. Simple and cheap!

Plastic clip and lock food containers
Reduction No. 29
I know this is plastic, but at least clip and lock containers are reusable. I have these in all shapes and sizes, and use them in the fridge, freezer, and for taking food on picnics too. You can wash and use these repeatedly, so they last a long time. The only downside is that if you store a tomato-based sauce or something that contains turmeric in them, they do stain, so try to avoid this if you can.

Other items
I see that a company based in Melbourne, Australia is about to launch a reusable cling wrap that you can cover food with either directly or over a bowl or plate. Apparently, you can even cook, bake or steam with it, using it in exactly the same way as baking paper or aluminium foil. It will be interesting to see if this becomes available in the UK, and if

so, how much it will cost. Although, I'm not sure I want to buy any more plastic items, multi-use or otherwise.

Aluminium foil
This is an alternative to clingfilm, but I only use this very rarely for the reasons I mentioned in the introduction.

Food leftovers

There are several items I haven't yet mentioned when talking about covering food.

Aluminium foil and foil trays
Reduction No. 30
If I don't use the clip and lock reusable plastic containers, I use aluminium foil trays for storing food for the freezer, usually dishes like shepherd's pie, curry etc.

For some reason I have quite a lot of these left over from when I lived on a smallholding and froze a lot of the produce I couldn't use fresh. This has the added benefit of being able to put the dish directly into the oven (once the food is defrosted).

These are quite cheap from the supermarket or from Amazon if you want to use them. Alternatively, and what I use more often now, is to store leftover food in an oven / freezer proof dish. This does the same job, but without the expense to the pocket and the environment.

Bread bags

Reduction No. 31

I make my own bread (in a bread-maker), which is so easy. You just put in all the ingredients into the cooking container (it takes about five minutes); put it on when you go to work, and then come home in the evening to the smell of freshly baked bread. Lovely!

You can control what ingredients go into the bread and play around with the recipe until you find something you really like. I used to store my bread in a plastic bag! Not anymore. I now have a bread bag, which although has a plastic insert, is washable and therefore reusable.

Cleaning the kitchen

When I was looking for all the plastic around the house, it was astonishing to find so much of the plastic in the cleaning products we use. My kitchen cleaning cupboard was full of it. Not only spray bottles, but also the 'quick' impregnated cloths that you can buy to clean work surfaces and windows. Sponges and disposable cloths contain plastic and are wrapped in this too.

I needed to find a way to reduce all of this plastic and here's what I did.

Cleaning cloths

Reduction No. 32

I used to use disposable cloths made of and wrapped in plastic. Now I buy reusable cloths and wash them in the washing machine. You have to be careful though because some of these cloths still come in packs wrapped in plastic. If I need to buy any new ones, I try to source these from companies that wrap them in a card container. The refill shop actually sells these singly, so I tend to buy these from there if I need a new one.

If I had more time I'd make my own cloths from old bits of towel, but I'll leave that to people who are much better at sewing than I am! Is this you?

Scourers and sponges

Reduction No. 33
I used to use the plastic and sponge scourers and have tried several non-plastic products to replace these. This included a brush, which was too harsh and too hard, and a Hessian scourer, which went limp in the middle and didn't really do the job properly.

I've now been trying a natural loofah sponge or Luffa cylindrica, to give it its proper botanic name. The Luffa is a fruit that is a member of the cucumber family. People in Asia often eat this as a vegetable. However, if the fruit ripens and dries on the vine, you can remove the peel, leaving the fibrous skeleton, which is the loofah we use for cleaning.

This comes flat packaged, but as soon as it goes into water, it puffs up and so was too big to use as a scourer. I got round this by cutting the loofa into three along its length, and just used a small amount of this. It worked perfectly, so I'll be using that from now on. I also get three scourers for the price of one (so just like buying a packet of three sponges)!

Kitchen cleaning products

If you look into my kitchen cupboard, you'll still find a whole heap of plastic cleaning bottles. However, I haven't actually bought a product from the supermarket for some time.

I've completely changed my cleaning products, mainly by making them myself. I wash out the old cleaning bottles and put my home-made cleaner into these. This makes the plastic container into a multi-use one rather than single. The benefit of plastic lasting hundreds of years is that it will be good for my cleaning products for some time to come. I have removed the old labels and now use a permanent marker to distinguish one product from the other.

I bought a few ingredients and these make up most of my cleaning fluids. This includes white vinegar and bicarbonate of soda. I've bought a couple of essential oils – lemon, rose geranium and rosemary to make the products smell nicer. I've also used fresh lemon juice too for cutting through any grease. I have lemons delivered from Riverford or Able and Cole when I need them (and when they are available).

Reduction No. 34
I now use white vinegar, bicarbonate of soda and lemon essential oil (or lemon juice) for general cleaning.

If you want to try this too, the ratios are:

- 50 ml white vinegar
- 5 tsp bicarbonate of soda
- 500 ml water
- 10 drops lemon essential oil (or a squeeze of lemon juice)

Mix everything together and put into a spray bottle. Don't forget to mark the spray bottle with what it is. This cleans really well. It smells a bit of vinegar when your first apply it, but his doesn't last long, particularly if you rinse it off with warm water. It's a lot cheaper than ready-made cleaner, as the ingredients last for a long time, so you can make a few bottles of this.

Reduction No. 35
I use rose geranium oil and water for polish.

If you want to try this too, the recipe is:

- 100 ml warm water
- Few drops of rose geranium essential oil

Mix these two together and put into a spray bottle. Spray onto a cloth to wipe over surfaces. Buff up with a dry cloth.

Kitchen roll

Kitchen roll, of course, is made of paper with a cardboard insert, and is therefore biodegradable. However, it usually comes wrapped in plastic.

Reduction No. 36

I looked into this and found a couple of companies selling kitchen roll without plastic. The first was Who Gives a Crap Forest Friendly Bamboo & Sugarcane Kitchen Towels. The company makes these from sustainable bamboo and sugarcane and it comes wrapped in recyclable paper. An added bonus is that the company donates 50% of the profits to help build toilets for people who need them around the world. However, the quality didn't come up to scratch, falling apart no sooner than it got slightly wet. It didn't tear at the perforations very well either and these seemed to be rather ad hoc. Perhaps they need to sharpen or change their perforation blades!

Reduction No. 37

I therefore searched for another, more robust option and I found one, Cheeky Panda kitchen towels. These are similar to the old ones I used so are much better.

The only problem is that if you buy these as individual packs, they come wrapped in plastic. However, when I looked into this further, I found that you can actually buy these direct from the company in bulk and plastic-free. This means the company sends these out in a recyclable cardboard box without a bit of plastic in sight.

What's even better is that they do a household sized bundle, which contains two kitchen rolls, six toilet rolls, and a box of tissues – perfect! I now buy these regularly, although over the Christmas period, as I had a house full of guests, I bought a box of 24 toilet rolls and a box of 10 kitchen rolls to see me through.

Rubbish

I think most people are used to recycling now and I try to make sure the correct items go into the correct bin. I have a two-section bin in my kitchen. One for recycling (our local waste collection service doesn't require us to sort out the recycling), which should go into the recycling bin without a bag, and another for landfill waste, which does need to be in a bag.

However, I sometimes get confused as to which items should go into which bin, especially if it says it is biodegradable, and of course, every council has different rules about what recycling products it will accept.

If you have trouble with this too, I have put a handy guide into appendix 1 to help you decide which bin to put your empty containers into.

Reduction No. 38

Unfortunately, our council wants us to put landfill waste into a bag so they can fester in the landfill site for the next 100 years or so! As rubbish bags are generally made of plastic, I wanted to find a plastic-free alternative. Although I found this area tricky, I did find a solution.

We have a food waste bin that council collects (I think it goes to a local digester to produce energy). However, in our kitchen we put all of our food waste, e.g. peelings, bones, fruit peel, etc. into a food caddy. We line this bin with a compostable bag, which we then throw into the food bin for our kerbside waste service to collect.

When I was looking for non-plastic rubbish bags for the landfill bin, I had a sudden thought. They do the same compostable bags in larger sizes so why don't I use these for the landfill bin as well. That way these will compost down much more quickly reducing the amount of plastic blowing around the environment. I did a trial to see if they would work and if the waste service would accept these. They did, so that's what we use now.

Window and mirror cleaners

Reduction No. 39

I used to use impregnated window cleaning cloths, but these are made of and wrapped in plastic. I've now stopped buying these and use my own home-made window cleaning fluid made with water, white vinegar and lemon essential oil.

If you want to try this out, the recipe is:

- 500 ml water
- 30 ml white vinegar
- Few drops of lemon and rosemary essential oil

Mix everything together and put into a spray bottle as usual. Just spray the windows with the liquid and wipe over with a soft reusable cloth. Dry off with newspaper. I remember my dad doing this 'in the old days'!

Washing-up liquid

Reduction No. 40

I still buy washing-up liquid. I use Ecover, but instead of buying individual bottles, I buy this in bulk, in five-litre containers. When I was looking into whether this reduced my plastic consumption, the internet said that buying in bulk used far less plastic than buying an individual bottle from the supermarket. Not wanting to completely rely on the internet for all my information, I actually did some calculations. Well, I didn't. I got my very bright niece to do this for me.

By working out the circumference of the 5 litre bottle and a 450 ml bottle (the size I used to buy) she did some very interesting maths (which I can't begin to understand) and calculated that by buying the five-litre bottle instead of the equivalent 11 x 450 ml bottles I was using 380% less plastic. A great reduction!

The alternative would be to refill the washing-up liquid bottles with Ecover at one of its refill stations. However, as my nearest refill point is about 18 miles away, having to use my car to refill a 450 ml bottle of washing-up liquid isn't particularly good for the rest of the environment! So the bulk purchase is my best option at the moment. I'm looking into alternatives, and I think my refill shop sells washing up liquid, so when I finish the 5 litre container, I'll investigate that option.

Dishwasher tablets

Reduction No. 41

I had been using Finish dishwashing tablets since I first had a dishwasher – whatever version gave me largest quantities for a decent price. The dishwasher manufacturers recommend using Finish, but some of these tablets are so expensive. In addition, and unfortunately, these also come in a plastic packet with each tablet wrapped in plastic too. Whilst these dissolve in water, I'm not sure whether they leave micro-plastics in the environment.

Whilst looking into alternatives, I found a dishwasher tablet that comes in a cardboard box, and although each tablet looks plastic wrapped, they aren't. This natural material breaks down quickly in water.

I have now been using Ecoleaf dishwasher tablets for some time, and the tablets are just as efficient as the big brands. I suppose it is the difference between buying Bird's Eye Peas, and the supermarket own brand that are often just as good as the big brands.

The downside is that local supermarkets don't stock these. I have to buy them online, but there are some great stores out there. I buy these tablets from the Ethical Superstore.

These are often cheaper than the big brands, so why not go for these instead and reduce your plastic use.

Laundry

Reduction No. 42
I used Ecover laundry liquid for many years, but I've changed the way I do my laundry now. I've started using laundry soap nuts. They are natural and organic.

You put four or five nuts into a little bag (which is supplied), and put these into the washing machine. They smell lovely and wash the clothes really well. You just dry the nuts off and you can use them again for four or five additional washes.

Reduction No. 43
I did use bottles of Ecover fabric conditioner too. However, I read somewhere that conditioner stopped the water from penetrating the fabric. So I tried not using conditioner for a while to see whether I could get away with not buying it and reducing plastic. The clothes just got coarse and scratchy, and made them difficult to iron. However, since using soap nuts there is no need for this, so I have now reduced that plastic.

This is a much cheaper way of doing your laundry as the nuts last for a while and replaces both washing powder / liquid and fabric conditioner. Give it a go and let me know how you get on.

Reduction No. 44
I try not to use the tumble dryer for clothes. I prefer to line dry clothes in the summer and put these onto an airer in the

house to dry in winter (I'm not lucky enough to have a utility room). I only tumble dry towels to keep them soft, and underwear as these take up lots of room on the airer.

I found out that, like baby wipes, tumble drying sheets are also made of plastic, so I've stopped using those too. I now use tumble dryer balls that you can buy from Lakeland. Although these are plastic, they are multi-use and a good replacement for the plastic sheets I used in the past.

The marketing hype says that these reduce the amount of time needed for the items to tumble but I don't find this is the case. The towels and underwear still take as long as they ever did. However, the washing does seem to come out soft, so they do the job I want them to do.

Chapter 2
Reducing plastic in the bathroom

Although small in comparison to the kitchen (in my house), there is a large amount of plastic in this little room. This ranged from toothpaste and toothbrushes, shampoo and conditioner, bubble bath, shower gel, not to mention the cleaning products.

All this plastic had to go. Here's how I managed to reduce the amount of plastic in the bathroom, although I have to admit, I wasn't entirely successful.

As I've struggled in this area, I'm not sure I can recommend anything cheaper than what I've tried here.

Hair and bath products

Shampoo

Reduction No. 45
I have used Daniel Galvin Jr. Honeydew Melon Hair Juice (that's shampoo to you and me) for many years. Of course, this product comes in a single-use plastic container! My husband uses this shampoo too, so we keep a bottle in the en suite (which he uses) and one in the bathroom which I use), so that's double the amount of single-use plastic.

I wanted to make a change to reduce single-use plastic and there were several options open to me. This ranged from shampoo cubes and a shampoo bar, both of which are quite reasonably priced, to shampoo that comes in an aluminium bottle (we talked about aluminium earlier), which was much more expensive (see below).

As we have a refill shop in the local town (Refill Revolution), I paid them a visit to see what they had in stock and I found Faith in Nature shampoo in different scents. This is a UK based company that uses natural and sustainable, organic ingredients where possible.

I am conscious of the fact that in the refill shop, this shampoo comes in a plastic 5 litre container. However, it turns out that this is recyclable and reusable if you return it to the company. I now buy 1 litre of this at a time from Refill Revolution, which I keep in a glass bottle with an aluminium lid. I then refill both of our bottles up at home using the larger bottle. I can then just take the glass bottle back for a refill (even before it runs out).

The alternative shampoo I talked about earlier that comes in an aluminium bottle, is from the UK and uses natural ingredients. It is manufactured by a company called Kind Beeuty (no this isn't a spelling mistake), which was launched by Amal Clooney. The aluminium shampoo bottle is available with a pump, or as a refill with just a screw cap. As an added bonus, the company will also accept back your empties, and will send you a free returns label to enable you to mail this back to them. However, it's quite expensive at £14.95 for 250 ml, the reason I didn't go for this option.

Conditioner

As with the shampoo, I'd used Daniel Galvin Jr. Honeydew Melon Hair Juice Protein Conditioner for years. Again in a single-use plastic container, (at least my husband doesn't have one of these as well).

Reduction No. 46
To reduce the single-use nature of this and as with the shampoo, I now buy 500ml of Faith in Nature conditioner, in a refillable glass bottle with an aluminium lid, and refill the original conditioner container at home from this bottle. I then just take the glass bottle back for a refill (even before it runs out).

As mentioned with the shampoo, Amal's Kind Beeuty range also has a conditioner, which comes in a recyclable and refillable aluminium container. Again, it's not cheap, costing £16.95 for 250mls. From Refill Revolution, I can buy the Faith in Nature shampoo and conditioner for £1.25 for 100ml, so in comparison, the Faith in Nature version comes in at just over £3 for the same amount, so much better value.

Body wash

I used to use Simple moisturising body wash. The only problem, once again, was the plastic single-use bottle.

Reduction No. 47
So I switched to soap, wrapped in paper. I've never been a

fan of soap, mainly because in hotels I don't like the way the soap sticks to the sink in a slimy mess. To try to prevent this happening on the side of the bath, I bought a slatted wooden soap holder to put the soap on, hoping this would reduce the problem. The soap stuck to that too although there was no slimy mess!

After a couple of mornings grappling with the bar of soap and the soap dish, I doused the slats with olive oil (from the kitchen) to stop it from sticking. That didn't work either, so I abandoned that idea and bought a Hessian bag instead into which I placed the soap. This was OK, but the soap left my skin very dry.

Even though this was plastic-free, I wasn't happy with the soap, so I ditched this and tried to find an alternative.

Reduction No. 48
My next step was to Refill Revolution again. As with the shampoo and conditioner, this sold Faith in Nature body wash in bulk. I tried the coconut version. Unfortunately, as I had already disposed of the Simple body wash bottle for the soap trial, I didn't have anything to put this in, so I bought from the refill shop a 500 ml glass bottle, with a pump. Whilst the pump is plastic, it isn't single use, as I use this all the time now. I now refill this bottle whenever I'm running low.

I actually considered buying the bulk version of this body wash, as I worked out I could save £13 by doing so, and even more if I consider the refill price I paid (which was obviously more expensive than buying the product direct — the refill shop has to make some sort of profit of course).

This also meant that I could return the 5 litre bottle to the company and get 20% off my next order, saving me an additional £8.25 and making the equivalent small bottle, half the retail price!

The company also had a deal on at the time that meant I could purchase the 5 litre bottle with a 25% discount if bought it any time during September. Great! Except that it wasn't. When I came to buy the body wash, around the middle of September, it was out of stock. I filled in the note asking them to tell me when this was back in stock, and kept checking the online store throughout the month, to no avail. But, guess what! On 1st October, I received an email saying that this was now back in stock — at the original price, of course. Well, call me cynical…!

I contacted the company to complain about this and it sent me an email in return saying it was looking into my complaint. I'm still waiting for a response.

Bath lily

I've used a bath lily for years and never really thought much about it, until I was looking around the house at all the plastic items. I spotted this hanging on the bath tap. Of course, it was plastic too, but this was quite easy to resolve.

Reduction No. 49
I have several flannels I use when I go away for a couple of

days (or on holiday), they are more compact than a bath lily, so don't take up much room in the toilet bag so I started to use these instead of the bath lily. They are plastic-free of course, but require regular washing.

Reduction No. 50
Whilst walking around the Refill Revolution I noticed the loofahs. I wondered whether this might be an alternative to the bath lily and flannel, so I bought one. It's amazing to see it go from a relatively flat item to one that swells up to three times its size.

It was a bit scratchy at first using it with soap (as I originally did), and it wasn't very successful. However, I tried it with my Faith in Nature body wash and it was fabulous. The loofah changed from being scratchy to a lovely exfoliating 'sponge'. I'll continue with this, and just use the flannel when going away, as the loofah is even bigger than the bath lily.

Shaving

Not a particularly glamorous thing to talk about, but I do shave my legs after finding I was allergic to the wax they used in the beauty shop.

Reduction No. 51
I originally used a plastic razor with renewable plastic heads. However, I've managed to find an alternative version, courtesy of a company called FFS (Friction Free Shaving). They offer a ladies razor that is made of metal, along with a subscription to have razor-heads sent every one to four

months. You can even have your razor engraved – handy if you have a group of girls living together I guess! My account was set up to receive four heads every two months, but I've now changed this so that I only have four heads delivered every four months.

The razor is a little heavier than a plastic version, so it takes a bit of getting used to, but I haven't cut myself (yet) and it gives a really close shave.

My husband has a metal razor with razor-blades that he received as a gift, and I bought one as a Christmas gift for someone else last year too.

Dental products

I've had some failures in this area, although I have made some positive changes too.

Toothbrush

Reduction No. 52
Like everyone else I'm sure, I used to buy toothbrushes at the local supermarket – plastic, of course – and the packaging is plastic as well. I looked around for an alternative, and bamboo toothbrushes seem to be all the rage in the plastic-free environment, so I bought one of those.

The bamboo makes it biodegradable and it was okay, in fact, I really like this. Moreover, I can buy new ones at my local refill store. The only issue I have with them is that their bristles are nylon – so plastic! You have to pull these out of the toothbrush when you've finished with it; otherwise the toothbrush is not completely biodegradable. This is not easy to do, even with a pair of pliers. I ended up having to chop the bristles off, so there will still be bits of plastic left in the head.

I was concerned about the use of nylon in the brushes, so I contacted one of the toothbrush companies about this. The Humble Co. said that they only use nylon, as they have not been able to find a suitable alternative. They have looked into using boar or pig hair for the bristles, but as these are not particularly hygienic and they are a vegan company, they are not suitable. They did say they were continuing to look for alternatives, and as soon as they can find one, they will take steps to change the bristles. I guess this is good news, but I wonder how long this will take.

The only downside is that the toothbrushes are more expensive than plastic versions.

Toothpaste

I've failed miserably in moving to plastic-free toothpaste, although I have tried. After searching around for a plastic-free version, I came across Georganics tooth powder. I didn't hold out much hope for this and I was right. It is like brushing your teeth with a mouth full of chalk. I gagged a lot with this. It had to go!

Then I tried the same company's toothpaste, a minty one. Unfortunately, it was still like brushing your teeth with chalk made into a paste with a bit of water. I didn't gag as much but it didn't leave a minty fresh feeling in the mouth. In fact, it tasted ghastly!

Unfortunately, I've gone back to my 'plastic packaged' toothpaste, until I can source one that I can actually get along with.

The one thing I am doing is saving all my toothpaste products and sending them to a local TerraCycle® outlet. I've just found out that my local refill shop has become an agent for this recycling scheme, so I will take them all the oral care products and packaging to them for forward on.

Floss sticks

Reduction No. 53
I have been a bit more successful at sourcing non-plastic versions of these, but they are not great. The first I tried were Knotty Picks from Knotty Floss – an American company. According to this company, they make biodegradable dental floss sticks called knotty picks, made from sustainably sourced bamboo infused with activated charcoal. This, apparently, enhances blood circulation and helps to whiten teeth. The packaging says they make the handles from corn starch suggesting that the floss sticks are completely biodegradable.

Unfortunately, having read more about this, it still takes many years to break down. I tried one and it nearly fell to bits at my first attempt. The floss stretched considerably when I first used it. In addition, the head isn't deep enough, which made it difficult to get to the bottom of the tooth.

Unfortunately, having researched further into this, the only other option is to buy a 'plastic' floss holder (there doesn't seem to be a metal one available in the UK), and purchase floss to use with it. At least the holder is not single use.

I've resorted to buying floss instead in a glass jar with an aluminium cap, but I don't particularly like this product, as it's too thin and weak.

Inter-dental brushes

This hasn't been much more successful, but I have found an acceptable alternative.

I used to use TePe inter-dental brushes, but these are plastic, so wanted to find a plastic-free version. The first variety I bought was inter-dental brushes from The Humble Co. These have bamboo handles (although still nylon brushes).

I chose the same sizes as the TePe brushes, as these were in millimetres – and hoped the sizes would be comparable. However, I did learn (once again) that you should never assume anything! The smaller brushes didn't fit the gap between my teeth and bent at the first attempt and once bent, I couldn't seem to use them any further. I used two brushes in two days, whereas the TePe's can last a bit longer with a good clean after each use.

Reduction No. 54

I found another non-plastic inter-dental brush variety. Piksters, so I tried them and these are much better. Again, they have bamboo handles (and nylon brushes). The sizes were a little difficult to compare to TePe's but the ones that I picked were comparable to these and they are much more robust than The Humble Co. version. So I will continue with these until I can source a true plastic-free inter-dental brush alternative.

Other bathroom essentials

Deodorant

I've used a roll-on antiperspirant deodorant for years. The last product before I switched was Dove's Invisible Roll-on. I don't use this anymore.

When looking into the different 'plastic-free' options available, I came across a number of articles about antiperspirant. These said that they contained aluminium salts that clogged up the pores, stopping the skin from breathing and allowing the natural sweat to evaporate.

In addition, aluminium salts have had a bad press, supposedly causing all sorts of problems from Alzheimer's disease to breast cancer. There is no research to back this up though, and would require the skin to absorb vast quantities to cause these problems. Nevertheless, I thought it might be an idea to just use plain old deodorant and to see how this went.

Reduction No. 55

I now use a deodorant stick. I've tried two brands to date, one is very good, and this I now use regularly. The other one I tried was not so good. Both are natural and come in cardboard biodegradable tubes.

The one that wasn't a good buy was by Ku.tis and the reason I didn't like it was that it went onto the skin in bits, with most of the bits falling onto the floor or into the sink. It was quite gloopy and the last lump fell out of the tube well before I was near the end. I wasn't able to get this back into the tube to use, so about a third of this product was wasted.

The one I first tried and now use regularly is by Earth Conscious and is an award-winning deodorant, which comes in several different scents. I've tried a couple of these now, and have taken to the tea tree and lavender version. It's made on the Isle of Wight so doesn't have far to travel and 10p of each sale go to the Marine Conservation Society. It goes on smoothly and doesn't fall to bits as soon as you use it. I would recommend this if you are going to switch to a more environmentally friendly deodorant.

The downside to this is that this deodorant (and many similar types) are incredibly expensive compared to the Dove one I used to buy. They are about 3-4 times the price! These companies need to reduce this price if they want more people to buy these products.

Toilet paper

An essential product, I'm sure you'll agree, and I'm very

particular about this, having tried many brands over the last few years. Most toilet paper seems to be too flimsy these days. I don't remember this in the past, so I don't know whether this is a pricing issue. However, the paper and card tube isn't the main problem as this is essentially biodegradable. No, it's just that toilet rolls usually come wrapped in plastic.

I've now tried a couple of products that are plastic-free.

Reduction No. 56
The first is a toilet roll called Who Gives a Crap, a great sounding product, and wrapped in biodegradable paper. I mentioned this product when I talked about kitchen roll. However, this isn't a robust toilet paper so this got the thumbs down from me.

Reduction No. 57
The next toilet roll I tried is the one I now use, which is the Cheeky Panda range. The company makes this from sustainable and fast-growing bamboo (not the type that the bear eats). The only problem with this product is that it comes wrapped in plastic. Apparently, they treat the plastic with D2W and have tested this to find that there is 91% bio-degradation within 24 months, which doesn't degrade into micro-plastics, but food for bacteria and fungi. In addition to this, it can be recycled, but not all local councils will accept this type of plastic. I was a bit dubious about this.

However, I've found a solution to the problem, which I mentioned earlier. On the Cheeky Panda website, you can

buy bulk items that are delivered loose in a cardboard box —
so without the plastic wrapping (which they are promising
to get rid of over the next few years anyway).

You can also subscribe to receive the plastic-free bundle
(that I mentioned earlier) anywhere between weekly and six
monthly and receive a 5% discount on the usual price of
£10.

I bought one box and made a note to see how long it would
last, as I wanted to take out a subscription and get my
discount. Although typically, my supplies lasted three weeks
(not the one week, two weeks, one month or two months
on offer). I'll need to think about this. Maybe it will be
better to order two boxes every month. Maybe it will be
better to buy a bulk box of each every two to three months.
Who knows, I'll have to test this out.

Note: Cheeky Panda seem to have taken all their bundles
off sale during the coronavirus pandemic — I've emailed
them to find out why.

Hand wash

Reduction No. 58
I always bought hand wash in single-use plastic bottles. I
preferred this to soap (as I mentioned earlier). However, I
needed to do something to reduce this plastic. I found the
perfect answer to this at Refill Revolution. I had them fill a
large 1 litre glass jar with hand wash. On chatting to the
person keeping shop, she told me that their hand wash — Fig
and Orange — was delivered in a large plastic drum, which

when empty is taken away and refilled by the company making the hand wash, returning the full drum to the refill shop.

I returned home with the hand wash, and refilled all my current hand wash plastic bottles from the glass jar. Therefore, my single use plastic bottles have now all become multi-use.

Bathroom cleaners

Reduction No. 59
I have traditionally used Ecover bathroom products, but as with the kitchen products, I now make my own bathroom cleaner using water, white vinegar, bicarbonate of soda and essential oil (using the same recipe as the kitchen cleaner recipe). I have recycled an old spray cleaning bottle, having washed this out first, and then mixing the ingredients together. Just be careful as the bicarbonate makes it fizz. The cleaner works really well.

Toilet cleaner

Reduction No. 60
I have reduced my plastic consumption by buying a 5-litre container of toilet cleaner from Ecover. The cheapest I can find this is £10.69. Waitrose is selling a 750ml bottle of Ecover toilet cleaner for £1.80. I therefore get a tiny monetary saving but at least there is not as much plastic buying it this way.

I need to find a recipe for a good toilet cleaner. Does anyone know of one?

Cloths and sponges

I used to use the disposable cloths to clean the bathroom. Now, however, I use a washable cloth, which came as part of the pack I bought (see the kitchen section), so I can't really claim a reduction in plastic here, as I'd be double counting even though I have reduced the plastic in this respect.

Chapter 3
Reducing plastic in the bedroom

At first when you look around the bedroom, there doesn't seem to be so much plastic, but, of course, this is hidden away in drawers. After a bit of a hunt around I soon realised that there was quite a lot of plastic in the bedroom, and some that I had no idea how to reduce. I've done my best with some of the products but failed miserably with others.

I'll explain my disappointment as we go through this chapter, but I have managed to make some positive and welcome changes.

Hair care

Hairspray

I have very fine hair so I need lots of hairspray to maintain my hairstyle throughout the day so that it doesn't flop all over the place. I have always used Silvikrin Maximum Strength (5) hairspray. Whilst the can is recyclable, I'm conscious that there is a plastic spray fitting and lid. I've been looking everywhere for a plastic-free hairspray to replace this, to no avail.

There are, however, plenty of recipes online for making

your own hairspray, which of course you can put into your own reusable spritz bottle. The only problem is that these contain sugar or alcohol (a waste of alcohol if you ask me), and with a high sugar content I'd be concerned that I would be a magnet for wasps, and whilst I don't mind these critters, I'd rather not have them in my hair and stinging my head!

I've resigned myself to using my usual hairspray and hope manufacturers do something about the lid. I've written to the company about this and received a very prompt response, in which it said that its experts were working hard to reduce the unnecessary plastic in the product, to make this more recyclable where feasible to do so.

So whilst the company hasn't done anything yet, at least it is looking into this, or so it says.

Hair styling products

I use a hair mousse, usually Elvive (if I can get it although this seems to have disappeared from the shelves recently). Another product that I've not been able to find in a plastic-free alternative. It normally comes in an aluminium can, which is just about okay, but, again, it has a plastic spray nozzle and lid.

My internet searches for a plastic-free alternative, hasn't given me any options. What the searches suggest is not usually plastic-free, and often it's not even hair styling mousse!

I'll keep looking though.

Hairbrushing

I have a couple of plastic hairbrushes, a round one that I use when I dry my hair and one for making it look reasonable afterwards. I've had these for years and clean them out regularly, so although these are plastic, they are not single use. I do know that you can get bamboo brushes, so if all the teeth fall out of my current ones, or if I decide I need a new one, I will try out a bamboo version before anything else.

Cleansers and moisturisers

Face cleansers

Finally, an area where I've had more success.

I previously used Neal's Yard Remedies face cleaners and Clarins eye make-up remover. The Clarins product came in a plastic bottle, and the Clarins website made no mention of any sort of commitment to reduce plastic, so that automatically had to go.

Neal's Yard by comparison, has lots of information on its website about reducing its plastic packaging by 2025 (isn't that what the government is requiring anyway*). The facial cleanser came in a plastic tube, and I emailed them about this. Unfortunately, all they said was that they were passing my comments on! I've heard nothing since. Therefore, until it does reduce its plastic, I won't be buying any more products from them, which is a shame for them as I've found an alternative, and probably won't return if they do change.

*The government's strategy *Our Waste, Our Resources: Strategy for England* published in 2018 has an expectation *'To work towards all plastic packaging placed on the market being recyclable, reusable or compostable by 2025'* and to *'To eliminate avoidable plastic waste over the lifetime of the 25 Year Environment Plan'*. This is not very ambitious, and the reason I don't think Neal's Yard are actually trying hard enough.

Reduction No. 61
I now use Peace with the Wild Organic Cleansing Makeup Melt which the company makes using 100% organic and natural ingredients. It also comes in a recyclable aluminium bottle and lid with biodegradable label and lid liner. Although it is a little more oily than my previous cleanser, it leaves the skin feeling smooth and cleansed. It is gentle enough to remove my eye make-up with too. The only issue I find with this is that the bottle is too small, only containing 50 ml. Luckily you don't need to use very much of it.

The price is comparable to the Neal's Yard's products I used.

Facial moisturisers

Another Neal's Yard Remedies casualty is the Almond Moisturiser I used to use during the day, and the Nourishing Orange Flower Cream that I used at night. I bought these religiously for many years and although they came in a glass jar, they still had plastic lids. As their response to my email was disappointing, I don't use these anymore either.

Reduction No. 62
I have now switched to Peace With The Wild Organic Whipped Face Cream For Mature Skin. It comes with the texture of whipped cream, and although quite pricey at £20 for 50ml, you don't have to use much. The one I'm currently using has lasted me three months and I'm only halfway through. It is quite oily (although this is soon absorbed into the skin), but this also leaves the skin feeling silky and smooth.

Cotton wool

For years, I bought the Body Shop's Organic Cotton Rounds, mainly because these were made from organic cotton.

Of course, organic cotton grows without the use of synthetic additives or pesticides, and without genetically modified seed. However, it is not without its critics. There are people who believe that organic cotton isn't sustainable, because it uses three times the amount of water than conventional crops, which have far higher yields.

What they don't tell you is that the high-yielding cotton uses genetically modified seed (that still needs pesticide protection) and which does nothing for the soil compared to organically produced crops that protects the soil from erosion, flooding and run-off, and which, therefore, is the cotton I choose to buy.

Reduction No. 63

Rightly or wrongly, I have always been concerned that the cotton rounds contain plastic, but to be on the safe side, and to save a bit of money, I have invested in organic cotton washable make-up rounds. You can buy these from various companies, such as Peace With The Wild.

I use smaller ones for taking my eye make-up off (I have black and grey rounds for this, so the mascara doesn't stain the white cotton), and larger white ones for cleansing my face. I have a little net bag that I put them into when I've used them. I can close this up, and put the whole bag into the washing machine so the pads all wash together and don't end up sprinkled throughout the washing (which does happen if I don't close the bag properly)!

Cotton buds

I do use cotton buds, mainly when I've been a bit heavy handed with the mascara. I dip this into make-up cleanser and gently remove the unwanted mascara.

Reduction No. 64

I have bought cotton buds from Waitrose in the past, and these are been made from cotton and FSC sourced paper. However, they pack these in a non-recyclable plastic box. Therefore, I now buy Hydrophil organic cotton and bamboo cotton swabs in a card box, from Refill Revolution. These are 100% biodegradable and completely plastic-free.

Make-up

For years, I used Clarins make-up, and got on very well with it, except of late when they kept changing their products so that those I liked, would suddenly disappear. This is not the first time I've changed company because of this. I stopped using Body Shop products for this reason too, and that was at a time when I worked for the company!

Unfortunately, Clarins relies heavily on plastic for its product containers and around its boxes. As I had decided to make a change, I wanted to make this organic and plastic-free, so I had my work cut out to source make-up that fitted this ambition. I would find organic, but not plastic-free, or plastic-free that was not organic.

Reduction No. 65
In the end, I settled on Zao make-up. All its products are organic (certified by Ecocert), cruelty free and vegan, and are packaged in a sustainable bamboo casing. Inside this case, products such as face powders, blushers and eye shadows, come in an interior aluminium holder which, when finished, you can pop out and recycle, then refill the bamboo casing with a new aluminium holder. The bamboo cases also come with a cotton pouch in which to keep the products.

The only problem is that the mascara wand is plastic, and the refill includes a new plastic wand and insert. It's also not waterproof either, and smudges at the least little disturbance. I've tried to find alternative non-plastic organic mascara to no avail. However, this brand still reduces my previous plastic make-up packaging by a long way.

Perfume

This is another area where I've not had much luck.

I haven't changed my perfume brand for many years. My favourite is Coco Chanel, and I have a bottle of Chanel Allure that I use for 'posh' dos! That bottle has lasted me for at least 10 years.

The latter comes in a glass bottle, with a metal cap and spray fitting, although it looks as though the inner tube is plastic. The Coco Chanel is in a glass bottle, with a metal spray fitting, but the entire lid is plastic. I have written to Chanel to find out what they are doing to reduce their plastic consumption and they responded with a load of old rubbish as far as I'm concerned.

They started quite well by saying that they understood my environmental concerns, but their next bit was quite upsetting. They said they were measuring their environmental impact, but that they needed to find a balance between the aesthetics of its luxury brand and respect for the environment and that this was a long-term endeavour. I take this to mean that the look of the packaging is more important to them than the environment. I think I might have bought my last bottle of Chanel!

Tissues

I use tissues quite a lot. I have tissue cubes all over the house – in the lounge, in my study and beside my bed. I have a flat box of tissues that I use when I'm cleaning my face and putting on my make-up, and then I have a small 10-tissue pack in each of my handbags. That's a lot of tissues! My husband is always telling me to use a handkerchief but, being an ex-nurse, I don't like that idea. I think I have that slogan 'Catch it, bin it, kill it' ingrained into my psyche and of course, during the coronavirus pandemic, we were all being told to use tissues and dispose of these immediately after use.

Unfortunately, some of the tissues I used before had a piece of plastic surrounding the aperture. And of course, the 10-pack of tissues comes in a plastic pouch. If I bought a six-pack of these, that too was wrapped in plastic.

As I started to change all my tissue products over, I bought the Who Gives a Crap box of tissues. I bought this because, as with the kitchen roll, the company uses 100% sustainable bamboo to produce them and so they are biodegradable. Imagine my horror when I opened a box of tissues up to find plastic in the aperture of these too!

Reduction No. 66
I stopped buying them immediately, and instead now use the Cheeky Panda products, buying these in bulk. I can buy boxes of 12 cubes and 12 flat boxed tissues, without a piece of plastic in sight. Now, instead of buying the 10-packs of

tissues, I just fold up four or five of these tissues, and keep these in a little pouch in my handbag, although the company now produces these in a little cardboard container.

Hand and nail care

Hand cream

Reduction No. 67

In the past, I've been very poor at using hand cream. If I do remember, I use any tube of cream I can find in the house – usually an old Christmas or birthday present. More often than not, the tubes are made of plastic. Occasionally, I'll find an aluminium tube, although not often. Now, though, I buy Peace With The Wild Organic Whipped Hand Butter which comes in an aluminium recyclable pot. It has a lovely scent, when I remember to use it, containing orange and vanilla oils, although it does smell a bit like chocolate!

Nail varnish

I do occasionally use nail varnish, preferring Jessica nail varnish for its long life. Unfortunately, whilst the bottle is glass, the lid and the brush are made of plastic. I can only imagine how difficult that is to degrade over time, particularly with the dregs of nail varnish in it.

Reduction No. 68

However, Zao offers a nail varnish that they make mostly from natural ingredients and this comes in a glass bottle with a bamboo lid like the rest of its make-up. The company guarantees that their nail varnishes are free from 10 harmful ingredients normally present in many nail varnishes. It is a bit streaky and thin though, so I would recommend a couple of coats.

Unlike all the other Zao products, at the moment there are no refills of the nail varnish but there are plans for refills in the near future, so that the brush and bamboo lid are retained.

Nail varnish remover

Reduction No. 69
I've been able to find several nail varnish removers that are virtually plastic-free and the one I've bought is, Remover by Fresh Therapies. This nail varnish remover is natural, biodegradable, vegan and cruelty free. It's apparently free from acetone and other undesirables so it doesn't dry out the nails. It's a bit expensive at £11.99 for 50ml, but as I don't paint my nails too often I think it's worth it, particularly as it comes in a glass bottle with an aluminium lid.

However, there is currently a plastic disk in the top of the lid and the label is plastic too. I wrote to the company, and the owner replied to say that it was a small independent business, so didn't have the resources to source and test lots of products. However, she did say that she was always on the lookout for ways to improve her products cost effectively, and that when she found the right items she would make changes.

This is a great response from such a small company. It's a shame some of the larger companies don't respond with such an honest and thoughtful answer. I hope that she will eliminate the non-plastic parts soon. Nevertheless, this is still a huge reduction in the amount of plastic packaging compared to my last nail varnish remover.

Chapter 4
Reducing plastic around the house

When I walked around the house with the purpose of hunting down all the plastic I could find, I realised that a lot of plastic is hidden within other products. It was only after doing a bit of research that I started to think critically about how I could reduce some of this.

You can't really class much of the plastic I found as single-use, but I still wanted to see whether I could do anything to reduce this. This chapter highlights some of the things I've done.

Clothes

I was horrified to see the amount of tiny fibres coming out of 'plastic' clothes when I was watching *War on Plastic with Hugh and Anita* on BBC1 early in 2019.

All clothes that are made of polyester, acrylic, nylon, viscose, modal and Lycra are plastic-based, and essentially made from crude oil and contain minuscule fibres that end up in the water system through the washing process. This adds even more plastic into our waterways and ultimately the ocean. In addition to this, the fibres can be detrimental to our health.

These fibres are tiny, much finer than hair, but are abundant in the atmosphere. A study published in April 2019 in ScienceMag.org, even found these micro-plastics in remote places such as at the top of the Pyrenees Mountain Range, showing that they are floating round the world on the wind. It is obvious that we are breathing these micro-plastics into our lungs too. Research is only just starting to look into the potential effects this could have on our health and wellbeing.

Reduction No. 70
For this reason, I no longer buy anything that is not made of the following 'natural' materials:

- Cotton
- Tencel
- Silk
- Linen
- Hemp
- Wool
- Cashmere

Reduction No. 71
Of course, I do already have clothing containing 'plastic' fabrics. Friends of the Earth (FotE) have offered some advice for reducing the release of these fibres when washing our clothes (although they concede that these aren't research-based). I have taken on board some of this advice. I now wash my clothes at the lower temperature of 30°C rather than 40°C. This less aggressive wash helps to reduce the number of fibres the clothes shed during washing. I now

only wash cotton items on a higher wash such as bedding and towels. I make sure the washing machine is full, which again reduces the agitation and therefore the number of fibres shed.

Reduction No. 72
One of the other things that FotE suggests is keeping the clothes for longer. I have therefore started to up-cycle my clothing – making something different out of the clothes I currently have before disposing of them. If I can't make anything new out of them, I take them to the charity shop so that someone else can use them.

Bed linen

Reduction No. 73
I've been decorating the house recently, and to match in with the changes in colour, I decided to buy some new bed linen. Whilst it's easy to buy polyester cotton products, especially as they iron so well, I have resisted the temptation, choosing plain cotton instead.

Decorating

As for the decorating, I don't normally take much notice of what brand of paint I buy, choosing the colours I want at the most affordable price. This time, though, I did some research into the paint before I bought any to see whether this contained plastic. It turns out that sometimes it does.

There have been changes in the regulations that cover paint recently to get rid of the harmful Volatile Organic Compounds (VOC) (the smelly part of paint). Regulations that came into force in the UK back in 2010, restrict how much of these can be put into paint.

This has brought about a change in paint products. So emulsion, for example, that is normally used for walls and ceilings, whilst is primarily water-based, also has vinyl or acrylic added to it for extra durability – i.e. plastic!

Reduction No. 74

My quest, therefore, was to find plastic-free alternatives. I found a brand called Auro, which is breathable, chemical free, emission free and plastic-free, but at £48 for 2.5 litres and £84 for 5 litres, it was rather expensive.

I carried on with my search, and found that Farrow and Ball was amongst those classed as eco-friendly, but only just slightly cheaper, it didn't say anything about plastic in their paint, so I emailed them and they said that their paints all contain an acrylic resin to help it stick to the surface being painted – so, plastic. These break down into micro-particles, which can enter the watercourse when you clean the brushes.

Hmm! Not sure I want to use this, just in case.

Of course, Dulux paint is half the price of these but also contains some horrors in its paint. I stopped reading when I got to carcinogen!

I carried on looking and found another company, Earthborn Paints, who sell an environmentally friendly and plastic-free paint, and is a little cheaper at £43 for 2.5 litres and £75 for 5 litres. I bought this paint instead.

Candles

I don't buy many candles for the house, but I notice that many of them come wrapped in plastic.

Reduction No. 75
When buying some large pillar candles recently, I found a small shop in my local town called Tiger that sold these without any plastic wrapping. There I was able to buy candles in an array of colours and sizes. I bought some white ones as table decorations for my husband's birthday celebration.

Mail and deliveries

I don't know about you, but every day, it seems, I get junk mail through the post. This is not just a circular that comes through the door, delivered by the postman (ours happens to be male), but those that are actually addressed to me, and which the postman is duty bound to deliver. Much of this comes wrapped in plastic.

Reduction No. 76
This is usually the result of some company or other passing my details on to others (without my permission). Now that the General Data Protection Regulations (GDPR) has come into force in the UK, if we want our information removed from their mailing list, they are duty bound to do this or they can face the wrath of the Information Commissioner's Office and a large fine should you wish to complain.

I have, therefore, been on a mission recently to stop all this junk mail falling though my door. I have written emails to the companies and asked them to stop. I have two stock emails for this (see below).

The first is to ask them to stop sending me information, reminding them that I didn't request this in the first place (just because I buy something from a company, doesn't give them the right to send me mail that I haven't agreed to). Then, if they send me anything again, I send another email that tells them that I have already asked them to stop sending me their junk, and telling them that I will pass their details on to the Information Commissioner's Office if they send me anything further. I keep a simple database of who I wrote to and the date of the email, so that I can refer back to this when something else comes through the door.

First email

Good [insert morning or afternoon],

I have received [insert what you've had delivered] through the post today, which I have not requested and I therefore assume you have my details on a database to which I have not given my consent.

Worst of all, this has come wrapped in plastic. As you know this is polluting the environment.

Please could you remove my details from your mailing list as soon as you receive this email, as I do not want to receive this type of information in the future.

Thank you in advance.
[Insert name]
[Insert address]

This is so they know who to take off their list.

Second email

Good [insert morning or afternoon],

I emailed you on [insert date] asking you to remove me from your mailing list for [insert what has been delivered], which has clearly not happened as I have received another mailing in the post from you. This is a breach of my GDPR rights. I request, once again, that you remove my details from your mailing list.

If I receive anything from your company in the post again, I will make a complaint to the Information Commissioner's Office explaining to them that you have ignored two requests to remove my details from your mailing list. After that, I expect they will be in touch with you.

Thank you.
[Insert name]
[Insert address]

Of course, you don't have to just limit these emails to those wrapped in plastic. You can send them to any company that sends you circulars you don't want.

Chapter 5
Removing plastic from the garden

The garden is an area where there is an abundance of plastic, much of it is not single-use, but some is. A walk around the garden (and the garage and shed) helped me to identify a few plastic items that I could try to reduce. This chapter explains what I found.

Remember me telling you that I bought organic produce whenever possible? Well, this is also how I grow things in the garden.

Plant food and fertilisers

I grow lots of fruit and vegetables, and have done so for many years. I'm an organic gardener, so if the fruit and veg can't hack my way of gardening, I don't replace them with the same thing next time. Whatever I plant needs to be robust enough to survive in my garden (just as it has to in the wild).

I have used organic tomato feed in the past, which comes in a handy single-use plastic bottle, but I stopped buying these years ago. Not only because of the unwanted plastic, but my tomatoes (and everything else I used it for), seemed to grow quite happily without it.

I'm currently doing an environmental science degree. As part of this, I was reading recently, that 30% of all the nitrogen we consume comes from the false process of using industrial fertilisers on the land instead of allowing the nitrogen fixing bacteria in the soil to do their job naturally (as in organic farming). A process that has been taking place for millions of years. This is a problem because this is effectively 'killing' the soil of its natural qualities. Another reason I eat organic food!

Reduction No. 77
We make our own compost. My husband's a whizz at this! We use the kitchen vegetable peelings, prunings from the fruit trees and other garden waste and from the next door neighbour's lawn clippings to make this, adding the odd bit of card and newspaper to stop the compost from becoming soggy.

This breaks down rather nicely into 'black gold' and we add this to the vegetable beds in the autumn/winter. This replaces the need to buy any fertilisers and probably accounts for the fact that my tomatoes grow quite well without additional feed. We do have to remember to water them though!

Why not have a go at making your own compost if you have room in the garden. If you don't have a garden, you could always buy a wormery, which you can put by the back door or on your balcony, (I used to have one of these too). Any kitchen peelings can go into this (not meat or fish). This will make compost for your pots and containers. If you are handy at DIY, you could make your own wormery. There are instructions for doing this on the internet.

Pesticides (bug killer) and herbicides (weed killer)

I have used weed killer in the past (which comes in a convenient plastic spray bottle), but I don't use these two products in the garden at all now. Even though the slugs eating my lettuces often make me want to reach for the pesticide! Instead, we use natural processes e.g. birds and insects like ladybirds, to control the bugs on the plants. Also, as we have such a small garden now, I can hand weed the entire garden in a morning.

I believe, nowadays, there are very few of these products available for the gardener to buy anyway, so we all need to get used to gardening without them.

Reduction No. 78

I'm a great believer in companion planting and have used this for many years even though there isn't a great amount of evidence supporting this practice. I plant poached egg plant (Limnanthes Douglasii) in the garden which attracts hover flies, lacewings and ladybirds (all of whose young are voracious eaters of greenfly).

I also sow French marigolds (tagetes) seeds amongst the tomatoes (when I remember them), which also helps to keep greenfly away. I also plant leeks and carrots close together as the onion smell keeps the carrot fly away (that and planting my carrot seed in a bed or pot that is two feet above ground, as carrot flies can't fly above this height!). I also run nasturtiums through my flower beds as these also keep greenfly and other pests away from the veggies.

Garden tools and equipment

Plastic garden tools are quite cheap and that's why I used to buy them. However, this is a false economy, as they actually don't seem to be very robust in the garden. They crack and break very easily with vigorous use.

I dread to think of all the bits of plastic that have chipped off these and been left in the ground during my thirty-odd years of gardening.

Reduction No. 79
When I had the need to buy a new fork and spade recently, I chose good quality wooden and metal tools that I know will last a bit longer in the garden than their plastic predecessors.

Garden twine

For some reason, I seem to go through a lot of garden twine. I use this to tie up flowers such as climbing roses, clematis and my favourite sweet peas. I also use it for vegetables, tying in runner beans and peas and for attaching the tomatoes and cucumbers to their frames.

Reduction No. 80
For some strange reason, in the garden centre balls of garden twine often come wrapped in plastic – why is this? It's not as if it has to stay clean is it, and it's not as though

it's going to unravel. I've spent many an annoying 10 minutes trying to find the end of a new roll of twine! The weird thing is that they also sell rolls without any plastic wrapping, so I now only buy rolls of twine that comes without its plastic coat!

I also make sure the twine is biodegradable, and doesn't contain plastic. I usually remove all bits of twine from supports at the end of the season and these all go into the compost heap. For this to break down into compost that I can use around the garden, it can't have any plastic within it.

Bird food

I do buy food for the birds, not that we get many birds in the garden. We live on a new housing estate, so this displaced some of the wildlife during the build. To counter this, the building company put some wildlife boxes up.

Our next door neighbour has a bat box in their garage roof, and we had a sparrow box on our garage wall (in a completely inaccessible place), until my husband removed this.

We have put up various bird feeders, a bird box and a bug box. We sometimes have birds in the garden, a wren, robin, blackbird and some sparrows seem to be the most abundant visitors. Although they seem to visit regularly when there are cherries and strawberries ripening!

There seemed to be a feeding frenzy in the garden the other day, as we had blue tits, long tailed tits, great tits and a goldfinch in the garden, and hopping about on the roofs around us were a few pied wagtails. What a marvellous sight.

Unfortunately, bird food is another product that often comes wrapped in a plastic bag.

Reduction No. 81
To reduce plastic, I sourced some plastic-free wild bird food from The Real Plastic-free Online Shop. They do both seeds and nuts for birds, which the company packs in Natureflex™ film rather than plastic, which we can put into our compost bin, as it is compostable and biodegradable.

Seed sowing

I use plastic modules for raising my vegetables from seed. However, I've had these for many years now, so they are not really single-use.

If I ever needed to buy any more pots for this purpose (which I doubt), I would replace the plastic modules with coir biodegradable pots that I plant straight into the ground with the seedling intact.

You could make your own pots. Just roll some pieces of newspaper round a glass and tuck in the bottoms. Alternatively, you could use the middle of toilet rolls or the cups of an egg box.

Insect and bird netting

When you grow your own fruit and vegetables, there's nothing more soul destroying than seeing pigeons eating your new pea seedlings or finding your lovely lettuces have disappeared overnight, eaten by marauding slugs. And, the sight of caterpillars crawling all over the kale can make you want to cry!

For this reason, I buy insect and bird netting to protect some of the plants from being eaten by these little critters (it doesn't stop the slugs though, as my lettuces have been eaten for the past two years, even with beer traps in position)!

So what did the pigeons do for food this year? They ate the leaves and buds of my cherry tree instead. Consequently, I had no cherries this year.

I do, however, remove the netting from the fruit and vegetable beds at the end of each season, clean off all the dead plant debris and use this again the following year. Therefore, it's not really single-use plastic.

This coming year, I have plans to make permanent insect/bird proof frames with netting to completely cover the beds, and which will be a more robust way of keeping the critters off my seedlings.

Plant pots

I often buy plants in pots for the garden and of course,

these do come in a plastic pot, and often this is a black pot. I now try to buy plants that don't come in black plastic, as this plastic can't be recycled, as I mentioned when talking about meat earlier.

Reduction No. 82
This year, rather than buying a variety of plants in plastic pots for an area in my garden, I bought several packs of wild flower seeds, mixed these all together, and planted these into one of my beds. This resulted in a riot of colour throughout the spring and summer. I think I'm going to do this again next year. In fact, I'll use the bee-friendly wildflower seeds my sister bought me for Christmas.

Chapter 6
Reducing plastic in the work environment

There seems to be quite a lot of plastic around the workplace when you look closely. I think my colleagues are fed up with me pointing this out, and talking about plastic and waste in general. However, because I do this, it's rubbing off on them, and they all do their bit by recycling and cutting down on their use of plastic too.

It's not just in the place I work either. I have my own home office, where I do all my writing. I buy and keep stationery for this, so I have two workplaces from which to reduce plastic.

Stationery

At my workplace, there are many stationery cupboards and just by glancing into these, I can see there is a lot of plastic. For example, brand new plastic leaves and files for reports. I do use plastic leaves, but I recycle these by using the same ones repeatedly. However, I am trying to be as paperless as possible, so use these less and less. In my own stationery cupboard, all the plastic items are reusable.

Pens and pencils

I have used the same brand of pen for many years. This is a disposable Staedtler stick pen – in blue. I'm very particular about writing in blue, which is to do with the rebel in me. As a nurse in the 1980s, we had to use pens with black ink (so they could photocopy the records if need be – or so they told us).

Anyway, once I had finished nursing, I never used a pen with black ink again. I would shun freebies at conferences if they were in black, but blue was a different matter. All plastic of course, all throwaway! In addition, I would buy my pens in boxes of 10, so I had plenty around the house to use, I also kept several in my handbag that I took to work, or used just when I needed a pen.

Reduction No. 83
I have recently changed my pens to reusable and refillable Parker pens (both with blue ink)! I have a normal ball point pen and a rollerball pen (which I think I stole from my husband). I just need to buy refills for these. This is a reduction in the throwaway plastic of the Staedtler pen.

I was just a little concerned about how recyclable they were particularly as each refill has a little blue plastic cap at the top of the pen and the packaging contained plastic too. I therefore wrote to the company to find out what plans it had for reducing this. Its response was rather dismissive. It said that it valued sustainability, but as the pens couldn't go into the recycling bin, it recommended signing up to the TerraCycle® programme.

It doesn't look like they are even attempting to solve the plastic problem. Is this another company that is resting on its laurels? I sent another email about this, which they promptly ignored. I therefore won't be buying any more refills when these run out.

Reduction No. 84

In addition to the pens, I also used to use a Papermate plastic retractable pencil. I preferred these to ordinary pencils, as I could never find a pencil sharpener when I needed one. You just twisted the bottom and more lead appeared. Again, I would buy these in boxes of 10.

In response, I bought a Parker retractable pencil, with a box of replacement leads, which is a much better option, except for the fact that the pencil leads come in a plastic box. However, bearing in mind what the company has said above, I don't suppose I will be buying any more of these. I'm very disappointed with this response, even though I have reduced my plastic considerably.

Because of the company's response, I now have several 'ordinary' pencils on my desk, which I use regularly. To keep these sharp, I keep a pencil sharpener on my desk permanently too, a nice 'old-fashioned' metal one.

Take-away drinks

Reduction No. 85

I mentioned water in bottles before. At my workplace, there is a water cooler. I have a reusable glass, that I refill regularly with this water (the company did provide glasses for this purpose originally but these have long gone!).

At home, when working in my study, I fill a jug with water and pop in some lemon, or orange, or maybe some mint out of the garden and keep this topped up during the day. It's refreshing to have a little flavouring in it, rather than just drinking plain water all the time. I got this idea from my sister-in-law when we stayed with her one Christmas a few years ago – so thank you, Sue!

Desk snacks

When I was at work concentrating hard on the business of the day, I used to crave something sweet. Unfortunately, we had a charity tuck shop, where it was all too easy to buy biscuits, albeit in small packs, and I often used to buy something to satisfy this urge.

Reduction No. 86
Now, however, I've stopped this, as 1) the manufacturers wrap these products in plastic and 2) they're not particularly good when I am trying to control my weight!

At home, if I don't buy these, I don't eat them, and choose fruit as an alternative (which comes loose in my box). When in season, we enjoy snacking on apples and pears from the trees in our garden. It's lovely just to go out, pick an apple or pear and eat it. They taste better than any you can buy in the shops.

We have a tiny garden, it's only about 7 m x 10 m, but we have two cherry trees, a plum tree, two pear trees and three apple trees. I've chosen minarette varieties that grow into tall columns (about eight feet high), and can be planted

1 m apart. I planted them three years ago, and we've had apples from all three trees, pears from one tree (although the other has pears on it this year), some plums and a few cherries. They'll only get better with age and it saves many plastic bags!

Chapter 7
Reducing plastic use when enjoying life

Leisure time is important for all of us. It helps us to maintain our health and wellbeing and puts our working lives aside for a little while. Of course, I still want to do my bit to reduce plastic and I've found many ways I can do this whilst relaxing at home.

Shopping

Now that shops have to charge for bags, the use has dropped considerably. Apparently, this is fallen by 90% saving a whopping 61,000 tonnes of plastic from ending up in landfill (or the ocean).

Reduction No. 87
My car boot is full of reusable bags. There is something for every occasion, and I use these whenever I go into any supermarket, when I go to the farmers' market and even when I go clothes or gift shopping. I have stopped accepting bags offered from shops, unless they are plastic-free.

As I've already mentioned, I shop at Waitrose, and they have recently brought in a policy so you can't buy 5p bags anymore. In addition, they have compostable bags for their loose fruit and vegetable (not that any of this is organic!).

The only time that I seem to accrue plastic bags from shopping is when Ocado deliver their goods which always come in plastic bags. Not great, even though these are returnable. But as they've just sold out to Marks and Spencer I have stopped using them anyway, choosing Waitrose home delivery instead. With them, you can choose to have the items delivered in plastic bags or loose in crates, so I choose the latter every time. In fact, I think this is my default option.

Snacking

I try not to snack in between meals. I fact, apart from the odd biscuit at work, the only time I really snack is when my husband has a bowl of something next to him on the sofa in the evening. If I think I might need something extra at work, I usually take a little screw topped plastic reusable tub with something in from home, such as nuts or dried fruits. Unfortunately, these usually come wrapped in plastic!

Reduction No. 88
Refill Revolution sells loose nuts, some of which are organic, that I buy. I use a plastic container from home for these.

Picnicking

We do lots of picnicking, especially in the summer. This might be to the park with the family and a few sandwiches, or a nicer picnic when we attend local events. We've been to several of the latter during the past year, which have included the Shakespeare season at Tolethorpe Hall, which is just outside Stamford. We go to one or two of the plays each year.

Our local country park held its annual Music in the Park event, where six of the local brass bands play anything from classical to popular tunes, and I went to this with my niece (it rained!). My husband and I also went to our Town's Party at the Wharf event with my sister and brother-in-law – the band Abbamania headlined, which was great fun.

Reduction No. 89
It's heartening to see people unpacking their home-made picnics, transported in reusable containers. I now do the same instead of buying this ready made from the supermarket.

This year, I prepared salad with prawns, salmon and crab, with some crusty bread. Then we had fresh fruit for dessert. I packed these in reusable clip and lock containers. I also have a handy six-setting picnic set, which although plastic, is washable, so that when I get home I can just pop this into the dishwasher and it comes out ready for use next time.

Drink straws and stirrers

Reduction No. 90
If you ever have a cocktail, why does it have to come with a straw? This year, I have refused the straws in several bar drinks. It seems as though bars are very slow to catch on to the need for plastic-free items.

A ban on plastic straws, stirrers and cotton buds was

supposed to come into force in England in April 2020, but DEFRA (Department for Environment Food & Rural Affairs) has put this back to October 2020 citing the coronavirus pandemic as a reason for this. I'm still struggling to work out why the department delayed this ban in the same month it was supposed to come into force (is this another case of big companies in the government ears)? So the restaurants, cafes and bars that have been closed anyway, will now be able to display these for an additional three months before the bans comes in. I can't get my head around this!

Birthday and Christmas gifts

Birthday gifts

I've been on a plastic-free gift mission! Over the last year or so, I changed the way I buy birthday and Christmas gifts.

Reduction No. 91
It started with my sister-in-law's birthday which is close to her husband's birthday. I was thinking about what I could get for their respective birthdays that didn't contain plastic and wasn't something that would be totally useless.

I decided to get them tickets to see a Proms concert of their choice at the Royal Albert Hall, in London. They chose to go to the *Enigma Variations* by Edward Elgar, which they then combined with a longer stay in London.

Then next, I told another brother-in-law (my sister's husband), that for his birthday I was taking him and my sister out to dinner instead of giving a birthday gift. When I gave him some possible dates, we also threw the Party at the Wharf into the pot, which is what he chose and we had a great night.

For my husband's son and daughter-in-law we bought them tickets to see *Harry Potter and the Chamber of Secrets* accompanied by a live orchestra playing the music, which they really enjoyed.

For my mum's birthday, my sister and I booked to take her to London for the day to a performance of *Let's Face the Music* – a tribute to the great musicals and right up my mum's street! I've also did similar for my niece and my husband's birthdays.

This saves on any plastic as I just prepare a 'card' on my computer with all the details on, and include the tickets if they have already arrived.

Unfortunately, many of the venues have cancelled or rescheduled these performances due to the coronavirus outbreak. For those cancelled performances, I will need to rebook something for a later date.

I could actually count these as individual reductions, particularly as I have tried hard to come up with things that I know the person would really enjoy, but I'll only count this as one reduction. I will, however, count Christmas as another reduction as this is much more challenging.

Christmas gifts

Reduction No. 92

I thought I would use the same principle for Christmas, but I've found this quite hard, as there are a number of children to buy gifts for and a lot of the gifts they would normally receive or are available for their age group, are plastic.

So, in many of the cases, what I have done is to buy tickets for the family to see a play. The children love going to the panto at Christmas, and are as good as gold when they watch the events unfold, joining in with the banter of the pantomime dame (and we're talking about very young children here. They've been going from about the age of two). I thought that the family could then enjoy a nice day out and create a memory, instead of receiving a present that they open and fling to one side whilst they open the next. *Shrek* is the play I chose as their Christmas gift.

In addition, Christmas gift 'days out' included *The Planets* by Holst for my father-in-law (we'll take him to this, so we'll get some enjoyment out of this too), a 1980s musical play for my sister and tickets for my sister-in-law to see the Grimethorpe Colliery Band. I also bought a jazz concert for my stepson and daughter-in-law, and *Lion King* tickets for my niece and her partner.

Once again, some of these have been cancelled or rescheduled because of the pandemic. I'll have to get different tickets with the refund money.

Gift wrapping

Following on from the previous section on presents, I think my gift selections will keep the need for wrapping paper to a minimum.

Reduction No. 93
As you can't recycle some of the birthday and Christmas paper on sale (particularly that which contains glitter or foil motifs), any birthday or Christmas gifts that need wrapping, I have used brown paper. I made labels for these out of last year's Christmas and birthday cards (that don't contain foil or glitter), tied on with raffia and coloured string. I've also used cinnamon sticks and dried oranges to decorate the packages. They look attractive (and smell great under the tree too).

Of course, I also use any old Christmas and birthday paper I have accumulated, as long as this passes the 'scrunch' test. If it scrunches up and stays in its shape, this can be recycled (as long as you remove any Sellotape and bows first).

Reduction No. 94
People often overlook Sellotape, but this is made of plastic too. To counter this, I have bought paper tape instead. This actually matches in with the brown paper quite well, and sticks perfectly. It even fits into my tape dispenser.

Greetings cards

Reduction No. 95
I usually make my own Christmas cards for the family. I had

done this for some time, then one year, I didn't have the time to do these, so I bought a load of 'family' cards, and it cost me over £60. I vowed after that time, not to buy them again. However, over the last year, I have been concerned that some of the things I use to make these from are not biodegradable and are actually plastic, such as double-sided tape, sticky pads to make the card topper stand up, and of course, glitter isn't biodegradable either.

I had a rethink about the Christmas cards. I heard someone on the radio recently saying he was painting a new design for his Christmas cards, and inspiration stuck. I took out my watercolour paints and card, and proceeded to paint my own cards. These were quite simple, with Christmas trees, multi-coloured baubles, holly, ivy and tree decorations.

I don't really have the time to make birthday cards from scratch, so in the coming year, I might use the same principle and paint a card suitable for the season of the birthday. If I make each one slightly different, everyone will get a unique design.

Alternatively, my niece's partner designs fabulous cards so I can always buy some bespoke, plastic-free cards from her (which I have done recently). She also designed the cover for this book. Why not see for yourself just how talented she is. You can find her on Instagram @Just a Little Something20.

Chapter 8
Reducing plastic when travelling

It's easy to reach for takeaway plastic when travelling. Bottled water is so handy – but so are water refilling points, which many coffee shops have signed up to. You can also download a handy app, called Refill and find out your nearest location. When I first used this, I was so impressed that all the coffee shops, the pub and the hotel in my town are all refill points. Of course, this is much better when you are out and about and need a refill.

Suncream

I haven't needed to buy suncream for some time now – I must have bought a job lot a few years ago, and I still have some left. That tells you just how much time I sit outside!

I am a great believer that we should actually let the sun shine onto the skin for about 15 minutes anyway before putting on any cream, so that we get a good shot of vitamin D, rather than resorting to tablets or fortified foods to get the much needed fix.

Reduction No. 96
However, I've already bought some 'non-plastic' suncream for when the need arises. Peace With The Wild, a company I'm getting quite fond of now, do a mineral butter suncream

made from almonds, by a company called Amazinc and it does smell amazing. It has an SPF of 30 and comes in a recycled card tube, which itself is recyclable.

Wet wipes

Reduction No. 97

In the past, I used packs of wet wipes on family picnics and outings until I found out that these contained plastic and did a grand job of blocking up the drains and sewerage systems, let alone floating out to sea to entangle the marine life.

I don't use these anymore. Instead, when I am going on a picnic (or anywhere else where there might be sticky fingers), I take a cloth or flannel, which I have wet through and put into a snap and lock container. This does the trick at wiping away any mess, and can be rinsed and re dampened in any toilet facilities, if needed. I also take a bundle of kitchen roll with me as well to dry damp fingers.

Ice creams

Reduction No. 98

When we are out, and if I want an ice cream, to reduce my plastic consumption I now only choose ice cream in a cone that comes from a vendor, rather than in a plastic lined tub. I prefer the malted cones, although you can't always get these. Some of the flavours you can get from those 'Italian' ice cream stalls are fantastic.

Of course, there is an option to make ice lollies at home, and I have done this in the past. I have a load of wooden lolly sticks in my cupboard that I can use, although I haven't made these for some time.

I have had a bumper crop of raspberries in the garden this summer. A lolly made from whizzed up raspberries, a bit of sugar and some water (sieved to get rid of the pips) sounds delicious. I don't know why I haven't made any of these. I'll give them a go.

Takeaway food & drink

I'm not a great lover of takeaway food, and rarely eat this now, as it usually comes wrapped in something plastic. The only things I would probably eat as a takeaway are fish and chips, pizzas or a Chinese takeaway.

Reduction No. 99
However, it's quite easy to make your own takeaway-style food, and that's what I tend to do instead. So I make fish and chips using the ends of our bread that I whizz up into breadcrumbs and keep in the freezer (you don't have to thaw this, beforehand either). I use this to cover cod (after first dipping this in seasoned flour and beaten egg, which I then put into the oven on a baking tray to cook and crisp up (about 20 minutes).

Along with my homemade oven chips and peas, this takes about as long as it would to go and buy fish and chips from our local shop (they cook the fish to order so we have to wait for this) and then bring it home again.

Haven't the prices for fish and chips gone up recently? We seem to spend about £15 on this easily. I remember when this used to be just a couple of pounds.

Reduction No. 100
My bread maker makes pizza dough in 45 minutes, so that's easy to do (if I can get my brain in gear and plan this in advance)! I use pesto (either red or green) as the 'tomato' base, which I always have in the cupboard (organic, in a glass jar with an aluminium lid), and I usually have some cheese in the fridge to grate over the top. You can use anything as the topping, tomatoes, peppers, mushrooms, a tin of tuna or sweetcorn. It's also a good way of using up any leftovers.

Reduction No. 101
Occasionally, when we go for a picnic there is a bar nearby where you can get a drink. The trouble is that they usually service their drinks in a plastic 'glass' for safety reasons, as these won't break leaving glass everywhere for people to sit on.

I prefer to take my own drinks, although I will concede that for one of my picnics this summer, I bought ready prepared Pimm's and lemonade in cans, which of course can be recycled, but do contain plastic.

On another occasion, I made my own Pimm's drink and put this is a large plastic, reusable jug with a lid and took this with me instead. When we go to the Shakespeare plays, the auditorium (which is outside) gets quite chilly. Therefore, I usually take a flask of hot chocolate with me, rather than buying drinks in the bar. Lovely!

Conclusion

This book contains information on 101 different ways I have reduced single-use plastic. This doesn't mean you have to do this too, but it might give you one or two ideas of how you can cut down on the plastic in your household.

There are over 66 million people in the UK alone. If each person made one or two changes to the plastic they use, that would be 120 million fewer pieces of plastic floating about in the air, clogging up roadside verges or entangling fish in the sea.

Within this book, I have highlighted some of the organisations I have used to help me reduce my plastic, and I've outlined these alphabetically in appendix 2, so that you can benefit from them as well if you wish.

Good luck in reducing your plastic and let me know if you've found a better alternative to those I've mentioned in this book. I'm always open to try new items.

Appendix 1
What to do with your waste

What should you recycle and what should you not recycle? If like me you are often confused about whether to recycle something or put it into the landfill bin, here is a handy guide as to what to put into which bin.

Recyclable materials

You can place many materials into the recycling bin including **paper and card**, **aluminium cans**, **glass** (as long as it isn't broken), **cartons** and **plastic**. However, you need to check with your local council as to what types of plastic and other materials they collect within their recycling, as these vary around the country and some may recycle plastics that others don't.

In addition, items should be clean before recycling as dirty items could result in an entire load of recycling ending up in a landfill site. Why? I have no idea! Surely, they wash the plastic before making it into something else. Or is this just an excuse?

Companies that sell **batteries** (the equivalent of a pack of four AA batteries a day) must offer a free 'take-back' service. Therefore, most supermarkets will have a battery recycling point, so return your batteries to them.

Take small electronic items like **computers** to recycling plants to dismantle as almost 100% of computer components are reusable.

Some councils collect **small electrical items** for disposal. Our council has just started this service. Alternatively, why not try to get your electrical item fixed at one of the growing number of repair centres popping up around the country.

Biodegradable packaging

This refers to animal or plant-based materials that will break down more quickly than conventional packaging, when exposed to oxygen, heat and micro-organisms, returning the item to its natural state. However, there is no time limit on this, so it can still take a considerable amount of time to break down. In addition, there is the added concern that this uses precious growing land to produce plants to make the packaging material instead of growing food.

You cannot put these items into the recycling bin, into the food waste bin, into the garden waste bin or onto the household compost heap. Therefore, the only place you can put these is into the **landfill bin**, where the conditions needed to break these materials down cannot be guaranteed. So they rather defeat the object and some are seeing this as a supermarket cop-out as they try to address consumer concerns about plastic packaging.

Compostable packaging

Although it might seem that you can put 'compostable' items into your household compost bin, this isn't always the case. Household compost bins are cooler than municipal composting facilities, and so you should only put items that contain the **home composting seedling logo**, into the **home compost bin**.

You can compost other items that carry the **seedling logo** with your **municipal garden waste** so use that bin for waste that carries this sign.

You can view the logos at this web-page https://www.recyclenow.com/recycling-knowledge/ packaging-symbols-explained

Appendix 2
Recommended stockists

Abel & Cole
https://www.abelandcole.co.uk/
Online organic supermarket, specialising in fruit and vegetable boxes.

Amazinc
https://www.amazincskincare.com/
Natural skincare company producing plastic-free suncream.

Amazon
https://www.amazon.co.uk
An online shop selling a variety of items mentioned in this book.

Bees Wrap®
https://www.beeswrap.com/
A natural alternative to clingfilm. Available from Waitrose and Amazon.

Cheeky Panda
https://www.thecheekypanda.co.uk/
Sustainable and environmentally friendly alternatives to paper products, such as kitchen and toilet rolls and tissues.

Clipper
https://www.clipper-teas.com/

Producing plastic-free teabags and packaging.

Dryerballs
https://www.lakeland.co.uk/
Reusable tumble drying balls.

Earth Conscious
https://www.earthconscious.co.uk/
Produces natural, plastic-free, earth-friendly deodorants that are kind to the skin.

Earthborn
https://earthbornpaints.co.uk/
An environmentally friendly and plastic-free paint supplier.

Ecoleaf
https://www.sumawholesale.com/
Eco-friendly dishwasher tablets made using natural ingredients derived from sustainable sources.

Ecover
https://www.ecover.com/
Company producing environmentally friendly household products, such as toilet cleaner and washing-up liquid.

Faith in Nature
https://www.faithinnature.co.uk/
Providing natural, ethical body and hair products, such as shampoo, conditioner and body wash.

Farmers' Markets

The provision of local, often organic produce sold directly to the public. Check your local council for details of farmers' markets and dates in your area.

FFS (Friction Free Shaving)
https://www.ffs.co.uk/
An award-winning metal razor designed exclusively for women. Available in either rose gold or silver.

Fresh Therapies
https://freshtherapies.com/
Produces a natural nail varnish remover which doesn't strip the natural oils from your nails.

Hydrophil
https://hydrophil.com/
Plastic-free bamboo and certified cotton swabs, packed in a recycled cardboard box.

If You Care
https://www.ifyoucare.com/
Environmentally friendly paper-based kitchen and household products, such as food bags, parchment paper and recycled aluminium foil.

Mr Organic
https://mr-organic.com/
Organic tomato-based products including ketchup.

Nespresso
https://www.nestle-nespresso.com/

Provides coffee machines, and capsules that are recyclable.

Peace With The Wild
https://www.peacewiththewild.co.uk/
Provides and creates a large range of eco-friendly, sustainable and plastic-free products for all areas of the home, kitchen and beauty department.

Piksters
https://piksters.co.uk/
Provide a range of inter-dental brushes recommended and used by dental professionals.

Refill Revolution
https://www.refillrevolution.co.uk/
The shop offers a different way of shopping by providing a refill service of dry foods and household liquids directly into customers' own containers thereby reducing plastic packaging and waste.

Riverford
https://www.riverford.co.uk/
An organic box scheme specialising in fruit, vegetables and meat. The box scheme that I use.

Steenbergs
https://steenbergs.co.uk/
Provide a range of organic dried herbs and spices in glass jars.

TerraCycle®

https://www.terracycle.com/en-GB/
An organisation that has joined up with conscientious companies to recycle goods that are hard to reprocess.

The Ethical Superstore
https://www.ethicalsuperstore.com/
An online store that sources and supplies eco-friendly alternatives to everyday items that do as little harm to the environment as possible.

The Real Plastic Free Online Shop
https://www.realplasticfree.com/
An online store that sources and supplies everyday items in plastic-free packaging.

Waitrose
https://www.waitrose.com/
My local supermarket selling a variety of groceries and household materials.

Yeo Valley
https://www.yeovalley.co.uk/
Provide a range of dairy products including block and spreadable butter and yogurt.

Zao
https://zaoessenceofnature.co.uk/
A brand of 100% natural and certified organic (Ecocert) make-up, free from all toxic chemicals including parabens. Supplied in sustainable bamboo casings, the make-up is refillable, and thereby reduces plastic waste.

About Kim Grove

Kim has been a non-fiction writer for many years, having had over 100 items published in various media outlets for private, public and voluntary organisations.

With a keen interest on environmental issues, she is currently undertaking an environmental science degree with the Open University to learn more about the impact people are having on the planet.

Kim is taking advantage of this knowledge by finding new ways she can reduce her own carbon footprint, and writing about her experiences. She is then using this as a basis for encouraging others to reduce their environmental impact.

Inspired by David Attenborough's *Blue Planet II*, the documentary, *A Plastic Ocean* and BBC's *War on Plastic with Hugh and Anita*, she made plastic reduction her first challenge. This book focuses on the changes she made to reduce the amount of plastic around her home.

Kim has already made inroads on reducing her impact further, and has started the next book on becoming more environmentally sustainable based on these experiences.

Her website, www.earth-friendly-living.co.uk, is another tool for her to promote her efforts.

Connect with Kim:

www.earth-friendly-living.co.uk
www.kimgrove.co.uk

www.instagram.com/grove.kim
www.Twitter.com/kim_grove
www.facebook.com/kimgrove.co.uk

Acknowledgements

Thank you to Helen Baggott for editing this book for me, and to my husband David, and friends Mandip Bhasin and Karen Berkley for the many discussions and encouragement whilst writing this.

Thanks also go to Briony Cousins for designing the fabulous cover, and to my niece, Kara Hindwood for her maths brain, and her help and support when setting up the digital media outlets for the book.

Finally, to all the stockists for providing the reduced plastic or plastic-free items that I've been able to switch to. Without their foresight, the plastic problem would be far greater than it already is. Let's hope other manufacturers and retailers follow their example soon.

www.kimgrove.co.uk
www.earth-friendly-living.co.uk

Printed in Poland
by Amazon Fulfillment
Poland Sp. z o.o., Wrocław

61318847R00076